FinTech Women Walk the Talk

Nadia Edwards-Dashti

FinTech Women Walk the Talk

Moving the Needle for Workplace Gender Equality in Financial Services and Beyond

Nadia Edwards-Dashti
Harrington Starr Ltd.
London, UK

ISBN 978-3-030-90573-6 ISBN 978-3-030-90574-3 (eBook)
https://doi.org/10.1007/978-3-030-90574-3

This Palgrave Macmillan imprint is published by the registered company Springer Nature Switzerland AG
The registered company address is: Gewerbestrasse 11, 6330 Cham, Switzerland

The support my husband gave me made this book possible

Interviewee Biographies

I have interviewed more than 200 people in the industry for the Harrington Starr-powered podcast series 'FinTech with Nadia: The DEI (Diversity, Equity and Inclusion) Discussions'. This book is a celebration of all the women and allies I spoke to about addressing the gender imbalance in the industry. It is their direction and guidance of what more we should all be doing for gender equality in the workplace. I feel so privileged to have had the opportunity to learn from so many experts through their heartfelt journeys and experiences. The following people have all been quoted in the book and their contributions are about action—how we can all walk the talk for gender equality in any workplace.

Kimberley Abbott is Chief Executive Officer and Founder of Vested Impact, a groundbreaking FinTech start-up with a mission to 'redefine millionaire to be a person who impact millions of lives' through leveraging an impact assessment algorithm that enables people to make decisions on where to invest their money where it makes the best impact on society. Kimberley is also an Expert Consultant for the United Nations, leading the IT development responsible for assessing and measuring the effectiveness and impact of UN Peacekeeping Operations globally, and is also assisting the United Nations Peacekeeping missions with data-driven analysis to respond to the COVID-19 pandemic in the world's most vulnerable countries. Kimberley has been named in the 2017 UK's Top 50 Women in Engineering, 2018

Engineers Australia's Most Innovative Engineers, Australia's 100 Most Influential Women, 2020s 100 Meaningful Business Leaders, and JCI 2020 Top 10 Outstanding Young Persons.

Cecil Adjalo is a Director at award-winning Social Enterprise Foundervine and is the head of Business Intelligence at the rapidly growing Danish Tech Scale-Up Dixa. He started his career troubleshooting problems with hospital database software and progressed over the years into management consulting, start-up creation, and business advisory. He has worked for Accenture, EY, and Slalom on both large digital transformations to small technology strategy projects across a range of industries including finance, consumer retail, media, and more. Cecil has been recognised by Yahoo Finance and EMPower as one of 100 top global ethnic minority executives and separately by the Financial Times as 1 of the 100 topmost influential BAME Leaders in UK Tech.

Mary Agbesanwa is passionate about how technology is transforming the financial services industry and supporting millennials to achieve their full potential. She is a strategy and operations Management Consultant working predominantly with banks and FinTechs. Outside of work, she blogs on her Medium blog 'A Millennial's Diary' about careers and personal development for millennials, and co-runs a female millennial personal development and entrepreneurial community called Now You're Talking. Her recent accolades include being an MCA Young Consultant of the Year Finalist 2021, Innovate Finance Women in FinTech Powerlist 2020, McKinsey Next Generation Women Leader 2020, and No. 1 on EMpower and Yahoo Finance's Future Leader List 2020.

Aysun Ahi is the Chief People Officer at OpenPayd. She oversees talent acquisition, employee experience, and organisational design. Prior to OpenPayd, Aysun worked internationally and across several industry sectors in diverse cultures and working environments. She has extensive experience in helping businesses develop and execute talent strategies that foster growth, innovation, and organisational effectiveness. OpenPayd is a leading global payments and banking-as-a-service platform for the digital economy. Through its API-driven technology, businesses can embed financial services into their products and create the seamless user experiences needed to drive business growth. OpenPayd's platform removes the need to contract with multiple providers for different services and across different markets. Instead, businesses can access accounts, FX, international and domestic payments, acquiring and Open Banking services globally via single API integration.

Dagmara Aldridge is Chief Operating Officer at Zumo, an Edinburgh-based start-up that brings benefits of decentralisation and cryptocurrencies to everyone with their cryptocurrency wallet which makes buying, selling, and spending of digital assets seamless, simple, and secure. Since joining Zumo in 2020, Dagmara took the reins for business and customer operations. With her deep expertise in payments, she established Zumo's payment card capabilities which she also manages. Dagmara is a mental health champion and drives the establishment of an inclusive and psychologically safe company culture. Prior to joining Zumo, Dagmara spent her career in the financial services and payments industry leading change and delivery functions in high-growth blue chip companies and successful scale-ups. She is a Steering Committee Member of This is Me Scotland, mental health initiative fighting stigma surrounding mental health at work. Dagmara has passion for nurturing and growing talent, neuroscience of leadership and she is a fierce advocate for diversity and inclusion.

Julie Ashmore is a highly experienced senior leader, and has been working in the banking and finance market, in the UK and internationally, for over 35 years. She began her early career at Natwest in retail and then corporate banking, before moving into the world of receivables finance. She spent 13 years at Bibby Financial Services where she established a new venture in Poland, led a global change programme and took on her first formal Board roles. With a passion for innovation, over the last decade she spent 4 years at HSBC and has worked increasingly closely with FinTechs, developing new digital products to support lending to SMEs. In January 2020, she returned to Natwest, after a 25-year absence, to take up her latest position as Chief Executive Officer of Natwest Rapid Cash, an award-winning, market-leading digital lending business. Julie enjoys a challenge personally as well as at work; and is an adventurer in her spare time. She has skied to both Poles and completed 2 Atlantic crossings in the Clipper Round the World yacht race 17/18.

Henna Ashraf is a test professional with over 23 years of experience in the IT industry. Her passion for testing can be tracked back to her early professional years when she decided to make a shift from development to testing. Reason? She likes thinking like a user and making sure the products are ready for end users. The software testing industry is continuously evolving and she is excited for what lies ahead.

Dr. Wajeeha Hussain Awadh is a FinTech and digital banking expert and Chief Digital Officer at Al Baraka Banking Group. She looks after the digital transformation strategies and is currently engaged with several digital banking and FinTech projects. Wajeeha is considered the first Bahraini to have a Ph.D. focused on FinTech domain in Bahrain. Throughout her Ph.D. journey, she has been listed as Top 300 Most Influential Women in

Islamic Business and Finance 2019 by Cambridge IFA, ranked 29 world-wide and the first on Bahrain level. She was Head of Bahrain TechAwards in 2019 that took place in Dubai. Wajeeha was also a member of Women in FinTech Bahrain (WIFBH), an initiative by Bahrain Economic Development Board. Wajeeha has a number of international academic publications and non-academic publications in London and Kuala Lumpur. She has been speaking in more than 15 FinTech-related conferences and seminars locally and internationally.

Maya Aweida is a Sales Director at Nasdaq in the UK. Previously, she was part of the founding team at FinTech start-up HUBX where she helped grow the team, product, and market share. Maya has been recognised as a leading figure in FinTech on the Innovate Finance Women in FinTech Powerlist three years in a row. She has a B.Sc. in Economics and Management from Bristol University.

Sonya Barlow is an award-winning social entrepreneur, TEDx speaker, diversity coach, and author. Her businesses, LMF Network and SB Consulting, were founded to bridge the gap between companies and the community by supporting organisations to develop and implement effective diversity and inclusion strategies whilst building women's confidence and marginalised communities to achieve their version of success.

Randa Bennett is the Founder of vHelp; a reimbursement app supporting the third and public sectors across the UK by reimbursing volunteers quickly and securely. Randa immigrated to the UK in the late 90s and overcame significant cultural and language barriers to get to where she is today. She recently co-produced a podcast called An Immigrant Girl to talk about her journey from a shy reclusive young woman to the founder and public speaker she is today.

Chirine BenZaied-Bourgerie is Head of Innovation at Finastra. Her role is in 2 folds, in one hand, driving intrapreneurship activities at Finastra and inspiring Finastra's 10,000 people to innovate, and on the other hand, opening the innovation activities to the banks, financial institutions, and the wider FinTech ecosystem (start-ups, established FinTechs, incubators, universities, data providers, etc.).

Prior to that, Chirine was New Venture Development Manager, managing FinTechs partnerships for FusionFabric.cloud, Finastra's open development platform. And before that she spent more than 10 years in the capital market industry, where she held different roles in engineering, model validation, and product management.

Professor Sue Black is a multi-award-winning Computer Scientist, Technology Evangelist, and Digital Skills Expert. She was awarded an OBE for 'services to technology' in the 2016 Queen's New Year's Honours list. She is Professor of Computer Science and Technology Evangelist in the Department of Computer Science at Durham University, a UK government advisor, thought leader, Trustee at Comic Relief, social entrepreneur, writer, and public speaker. Sue set up the UK's first online network for women in tech BCSWomen in 1998 and led the campaign to save Bletchley Park, home of the WW2 codebreakers. Sue's first book Saving Bletchley Park details the social media campaign she led to save Bletchley Park from 2008–2011. Sue has championed women in tech for over two decades, founding the #techmums social enterprise in 2013 and the pioneering TechUPWomen retraining underserved women into tech careers in 2019.

Passionate about technology as an enabler Sue didn't have a traditional start to her career. She left home and school at 16, married at 20, and had 3 children by the age of 23. A single parent at 25 she went to university, gained a degree in computing, then a Ph.D. in software engineering. Sue now has 4 children and 5 grandchildren.

Kate Bohn is a transformational leader with 20+ years in financial services. She has delivered net-positive impacts across a broad range of roles in financial services. From global software houses to retail/investment banking institutions in the UK, Europe, and the US, she is at the forefront of both revolutionary and incremental change, be that through joint venture companies for industry utilities, leading the charge on emergent internet use in the 'noughties' or more day-to-day innovation that seeks to reduce complexity. A market networker, she is highly effective at both internal and external stakeholder engagement, as well as unifying divergent groups around a collective end goal. Her dextrous use of storytelling builds rapid understanding, connection and alignment, as well as embedding a sense of belonging into corporate cultures. Alongside her day job, she is an active mentor of the talent pipeline and currently working on a FinTech Leadership book for the broader innovation ecosystem.

Alexandra Boyle is a passionate FinTech leader focused on platform and ecosystem building in capital markets. In 2014, she joined OpenFin as one of the first 10 employees and has helped transform the global bank technology landscape. Her contribution to the industry has resulted in global recognition—in 2020 she was shortlisted for the European Women in Finance Award and named Banking Technology's Rising FinTech Star Alexandra also regularly participates in industry panels and events. Prior to joining OpenFin, she held multiple positions in product and business development at NYSE Euronext. Alexandra graduated with a Bachelor of Science in Finance from Lehigh University.

David Brear is the Chief Executive Officer of 11:FS and since his dream of being a sportsperson was crushed (along with the ligaments in his knee!) and he had to get a proper job, he has worked in pretty much every angle of the financial services industry never losing that competitive desire to drive forwards and win.

Having pitched, established, and run billion-pound transformations for some of the biggest FS companies on the planet the realisation that digital financial services is only 1% finished has spurred his desire to establish an organisation that can actually support the industry through its greatest challenge. 11:FS is a challenger to the incumbent consultancies. They create innovative strategies and build out new propositions and ventures in the UK, US, Europe, and Asia for some of the biggest brands on the planet. Alongside this 11:FS build in-house products from competitor benchmarking tools like 11:FS Pulse, to core banking and modern architecture systems like 11:FS Foundry.

Nicola Breyer has been passionate about building and scaling businesses for over 20 years, from the early days of the consumer internet to today. Her career spans roles as Co-Founder, Managing Director, Venture Capitalist, as well as Corporate Innovation & Transformation Specialist. Her industry focus includes financial services, FMCG, and media. Nicola headed up the Commercial Growth & Innovation Team initiatives for PayPal, based in Berlin. In July 2020, she joined OptioPay, an Open Banking Fin-/AdTech start-up as Chief Growth Officer and shareholder. At OptioPay she is responsible for B2B2C & B2B marketing, enterprise sales, platform monetization customer success, operations, customer service, international expansion, and general senior leadership tasks around team, strategy, and investor relations. Nicola is also passionate about creating positive impact in the world. She is holding board positions in for-profit social impact businesses (Vested Ltd. amongst others), supporting female founders. She is also an advisor to impact accelerators and funds like Village Capital and Planet a Ventures.

Sara Green Brodersen is a serial entrepreneur, having launched her first company when she was just 16. Since then she has started two more companies, including FinTech Canaree and ID verification tool Deemly. She has also headed up a number of community organisations focused on entrepreneurship and innovation. Danish of origin, she earned her M.Sc. from IT University of Copenhagen and has since worked in both San Francisco and London firstly as a management consultant and later as an innovative entrepreneur. She also holds exams from University of Cambridge and Stanford University. As an international public speaker, she enjoys sharing her passion about all things entrepreneurship and start-ups. She is actively involved in London's start-up and technology scene, and is passionate about inspiring diversity in the start-up ecosystem.

Anna Burgess started her IT career 20 years ago, with her first job providing 1st line technical support for NHS users. She doesn't have an IT-related degree: in 1999 she graduated from The Russian State Pedagogical University as an English teacher. When she arrived in the UK, she decided to pursue an IT career rather than becoming a teacher. Anna passed 7 Microsoft exams and gained the MSCE 2000 certificate which helped her get into a software company who took her on without prior experience. She worked her way up to the Infrastructure Support Team before moving to an FTSE250 finance company to manage an international Service Desk team across 3 continents. She has been in the financial sector for 8 years, the last 4 with Close Brothers. She started as Head of Service Centre managing 21 Service Desk analysts and now, since returning from maternity leave in 2019, Anna is a Senior Service Delivery Manager.

Sylvia Carrasco is keen on challenging the status quo as a woman in FinTech. She's the Founder and Chief Executive Officer of Goldex, the first gold marketplace that uses smart order routers to always find the best prices from a variety of gold providers. This model brings ethical price discovery to both retail and institutional gold investors. With over 20 years of experience in investment banking and brokerage, Sylvia was part of the original team at Credit Suisse that developed the first electronic trading and algorithmic systems in the equity markets. After leaving Credit Suisse, she took charge of MF Global's institutional electronic trading team where she further developed new algorithmic tools, set up trading connections to new liquidity venues, and advised on the implementation of Best Execution policies as required by MiFID I. Always thinking out of the box and due to the changes brought by MiFID I, in 2009 she successfully founded the first FCA regulated firm in the United Kingdom to advise the largest institutional investment houses in both electronic trading services and Best Execution policies across multi-asset classes.

Sarah Carver has held numerous roles across financial services across retail and commercial banking, investment banking, wealth management, and financial exchanges. She has worked across a number of disciplines including strategy, digital transformation, and change management and is currently the global head of digital for delta capita, a global managed services, technology solutions and consulting provider. Previous consulting roles have been for Accenture and Capco and her client list has included the London Stock Exchange, Deutsche Bank, Bank of America, Natwest, HSBC, private banks and new market entrants, and FinTech start-ups. Sarah is passionate about customer-led propositions, digital enablement, and transforming ways of working and she has authored numerous articles on these topics. She graduated with a Bachelor of Science in Management Sciences from Loughborough University.

Tribeni Chougule a multi-award winner, has over 20 years' experience in technology across diverse sectors and geographies. She is currently Head of Change Management in Visa Finance (Europe). Prior to this, she led the Technology innovation team in London Innovation Centre. Tribeni has delivered multiple Agile transformations and managed multiple complex programmes and projects throughout her career including mergers and acquisitions. She is also a WBS Executive M.B.A. student. Her dissertation explores Responsible Innovation using fair and unbiased AI within the financial services. Passionate about inclusion of diversity and social impact, Tribeni is the co-chair of Visa's Women in Technology Europe network and a techUK Skills and Diversity Council member. She is a Cherie Blair foundation Women in Business mentor alumnus, Women in Payments, Migrant Leader, and a Visa mentor. She is also an AI APPG task force member. Tribeni has established a STEM bursary for girls from disadvantaged backgrounds.

Alia Cooper has enjoyed a tremendous variety of roles during her career, but managing change has been a consistent thread. She began her career in technology and was an early practitioner of agile change management; a skillset that stood her in good stead as she transitioned into organisational transformation roles. Having spent several years working in the asset management sector she then took a role with HSBC and has driven Financial Crime Risk culture change across operations, business, and compliance functions. More recently she has expended her responsibilities to lead an Employee Resource Group dedicated to the support of colleagues with disabilities. This opened her eyes to the wider challenges across the equity, diversity, and inclusion agenda; for which she is a passionate and proactive advocate. Alia is committed to improving well-being through reducing the stigma attached to mental ill-health, and manages her own mental health by spending as much time as possible with her pets, horses, and 2-year-old niece.

Felicitas Coulibaly is the Global Head of Inside Sales at Mambu. With a deep passion for empathetic leadership and serving the underbanked, she has worked within the FinTech sector for the past 5 years, at some of the most competitive businesses in the market, i.e. Finastra, Temenos, and Thought Machine. As a young woman in a senior role, Felicitas focuses on empowering women and POCs, and also works with London-based charities empowering young people in underfunded areas to move towards further education and employment. Felicitas cares deeply about diversity and empowering people from all backgrounds, whilst facing complex challenges in the day-to-day business life of the FinTech sector. She believes that ageism has impacted not only herself but many young people, hindering career growth, hence she enables her team and network actively by creating equal opportunities and creating a culture of constructive feedback and promotions based on merit.

George Coxon is Director of the Nano Foundation, Director of Appia, and Advisor to the Global Blockchain Initiative. Nano is the world's only truly global currency, designed to democratise the global economy and bring financial inclusion to the world over. A degree in Evolutionary Anthropology amplified George's natural fascination in social behaviours and what makes people 'tick', giving her a wider understanding of how efficient, decentralised digital money can empower and elevate the underbanked, and begin to replace a world founded on credit with a sustainable and fairer solution based on instant settled-value anywhere on the planet. George is clear that an economy that is open to all and empowers those that are marginalised, not only financially but also socially and politically, will be more robust and resilient. To achieve this goal requires non-archetypal leadership to be at the forefront of the challenge which is the future of money.

Céline Crawford is Chief Communications Officer at FinTech Smarkets, an award-winning platform that facilitates trading on sport, politics, and current affairs. There she also leads people, politics and sits on the leadership team. Before joining Smarket in 2015, Céline spent 13 years in banking/PR/IR starting at Dresdner, followed by Edison and finnCap where she advised PLCs and worked in Equity Sales. She served as a Non-Executive Director at ethical quinoa producer Quinola. Céline is an outspoken champion for gender and racial equality and at Smarkets helped pioneer forward-thinking initiatives such as transparent salaries to help combat the gender and racial pay gap. She is also a big advocate for Mental health in the workplace and created initiatives such as Tête-à-tête: a safe and open weekly session for employees to talk about their well-being, supplemented by the company paying for 75% of employee counselling. On the side, she is a mum and hosts a podcast on Mental Health called @15minsoffemme.

Nick Dennes has worked in Talent, Recruitment and Executive Search, Direct and RPO In-House roles at Marex, Man Group, KPMG and EY, in the UK, US, and Australia. She has been involved with account management, stakeholder management, strategic partnerships, and relationship development. A talent for developing partnerships across the business, client engagement, and winning new business. Passionate about networking. She was a previous Chair for 3 years of a London-based Women's Business Network (ELN). An avid Ironman triathlete who has raced 8 full Ironman distance races across all 6 continents, chaired a corporate triathlon club of 350 members, and been a Director for the London Regional Committee for Triathlon England.

Nilixa Devlukia is the Founder of Payments Solved, a regulatory consultancy advising on the regulatory framework for crypto assets, CBDC, payment services, and open banking both in the UK and globally. Nilixa is an experienced regulatory expert and lawyer with a Master's in European Competition Law and over 20 years of banking and payments experience gained from her time at Barclays, the FCA, the European Banking Authority, and as Head of Regulatory at the Open Banking Implementation Entity. Nilixa has worked extensively with the European Commission, the European Central Bank, the World Bank, and regulators across the globe. Nilixa has represented the UK and FCA on various EU and UK level committees including the ECB SecurePay Forum, the EU API Evaluation Group, and the UK Payment Strategy Forum and lead on the publication of the FCA Approach Document on Payment Services and EBA Consultations. Nilixa is a well-known public speaker and works with industry, regulators, and legislators to drive changes in the banking and payments ecosystem for a payments and open banking landscape that is secure, transparent, and inclusive.

Joanne Dewar is Chief Executive Officer of Global Processing Services (GPS), the trusted and proven go-to payments processing partner for over 180 of today's leading challenger FinTechs around the world, including Revolut, Starling Bank, and Curve. GPS has to date issued over 170 million cards—enabled in over 48 countries—and processed over 1.3 billion transactions through its platform in 2020. Since joining the company in 2013, Joanne has spearheaded the transformation of GPS from start-up to private equity-backed scale-up, cementing the business' position as the bedrock of the FinTech ecosystem, as it continues to accelerate the delivery of better financial experiences for every customer. Joanne is a recognised leader and influencer in the payments industry, having been selected as one of the top 50 FinTech CEOs of 2021, alongside leaders from Stripe, Klarna, Wise, Coinbase, Marqeta, and more. She was also named in the 2019 and 2020 Payments Power 10 list, which recognises payments industry leaders with an ongoing commitment to pushing boundaries in the payments sector. Under Joanne's stewardship, GPS won 12 industry awards in the space of 12 months, securing the highly coveted title of Best Processing Programme at the Card and Payments Awards, as well as being crowned Leading Emerging Payments Organisation at the Emerging Payments Awards. She was also named Export Champion by the Department for International Trade (DIT), a community made up of business leaders who have successfully sold overseas and are prepared to share their time and experience to encourage more companies to export. It forms a crucial part of the DIT's Export Strategy, launched in 2018 to increase the value of GDP through exports from 30 to 35%.

Sharon Doherty as a Chief People Officer of Finastra is a member of the executive leadership team and has global responsibility for making Finastra one of the most well-known and inclusive employers in financial services. She is committed to empowering people to help Finastra achieve this mission, and together with them, create a culture that attracts and inspires people to disrupt the financial services and FinTech industries. A passionate champion for diversity and inclusion at all levels, Sharon joined Finastra from Vodafone, where she held the position of Global Organization and People Development Director. There she was instrumental in the award-winning diversity and digital work that transformed the culture and company. At Vodafone, Sharon was a driving force behind Vodafone's award-winning diversity and inclusion agenda and was recognised in the 2018 Outstanding Leaders and Allies list. Sharon's previous experience includes role at CHRO at Laing O'Rourke and HR Director during the build of Heathrow's Terminal 5.

Rebecca Duckworth joined QV Systems as the Chief Sales and Marketing Officer after a successful 25-year career in digital banking, helping to revolutionise customer interactions for some of the largest banks in the US and Europe. With experience from Digital Insight, Intuit Financial Services, and Fiserv, Rebecca brings a wealth of expertise and knowledge in innovative technology like AI, Machine Learning, eID and V, and Open Banking, to help revolutionise the way customers can interact with asset, automotive, and consumer finance companies.

Ridhima Durham was educated in India and the UK, graduating with an M.A. (Economics and Management) from Oxford University. After nearly 5 years at Goldman Sachs, she moved onto a Hedge Fund of Funds called NewFinanceCapital (subsidiary of Schroders Plc). She started her journey in FinTech as Everline's Head of Commercial (London) then as Bond Street's CRO (NY). In 2019, she was appointed Chief Commercial Officer at high-growth scale-up Salary Finance. She is passionate about women's careers and especially encourages and mentors women in FinTech and is an active member of the 'Ladies who Launch' group.

Annette Evans is Vice President of People at Global Processing Services (GPS), the trusted and proven go-to payments processing partner for today's leading challenger brands, including Revolut, Starling Bank, and Curve. A highly skilled MCIPD HR Generalist and Employment Law specialist, with extensive experience in streamlining Human Resources processes and a mentor on the CIPD Skills Up programme, as well as a trained ACAS

Internal Workplace Mediator. Annette plays a key role in directing the entire spectrum of people policies, talent acquisition, performance management, and compensation. Working closely with the senior executive team, she has established clear company values and data-driven processes to inform people decisions and a purposeful culture to help companies achieve their mission of enabling financial empowerment for everyone.

Thea Fisher is a UK and US national based in London with a varied background in business to business commercial strategy, as well as early-stage tech investment and operations. She is currently Head of Partnerships at Academy, a digital training platform aiming to solve the gap between the supply and demand for tech talent. In her role, she focuses on commercial strategy, developing and managing relationships with key employer partners. Prior to her role with Academy, she was Head of Commercial at Littlepay, a micropayments processing start-up making everyday payments simpler, faster, and easier. She has a Master's in Economic History from the London School of Economics, and a Bachelor's from King's College London in English Literature.

Anna Flach is a Global Marketing Director and business leader with ten years of experience in investment banking and financial technology. She leads the Marketing & Communications function at BSO, a leading infrastructure and connectivity provider, and oversees all marketing activities across client segments to drive engagement, experience, and revenue. Prior to BSO, Anna held roles at Commerzbank, BNP Paribas and Allianz in London, Paris, and Munich. Following that, she took a leap into the world of FinTech, where she was most recently working towards the adoption of blockchain technology in capital markets. The UK voice of FinTech, Innovate Finance, recognised her for leading the change in the ecosystem for two consecutive years (Women in FinTech Powerlist 2018 and 2019). In 2020 Anna was nominated by Capacity Media as one of the '20 Women to Watch in Telco and Tech' and she was shortlisted for European Women in Finance Awards 2020. She is also listed as an official contributor to the Rose Review of Female Entrepreneurship. Anna speaks English, French, and German and holds a BSc in Business and Psychology and an MSc in Management from EMLyon Business School.

Alex Ford is Vice President of Product & Marketing for RegTech firm Encompass, and she oversees both functions globally from Sydney. She has held a range of roles since joining Encompass in 2012 spanning from Customer Success to Product Management. From 2015 to 2020 Alex was based in Glasgow driving the launch and expansion of the UK operation. As host of the RegTech 20/20 podcast she showcases industry trends and professionals from across the global RegTech community. She also serves on the board of The RegTech Association and marketing committee of the Business Information Industry Association. Prior to Encompass Alex worked in innovation and marketing roles for coaching, leadership, and technology businesses.

Debbie Forster, MBE is an award-winning figure in the areas of diversity, tech, innovation, and education. She is a portfolio consultant and coach and is Co-Founder and Chief Executive Officer for the Tech Talent Charter, an industry collective which aims to deliver greater inclusion and diversity in the UK tech workforce. Women in Science and Engineering (WISE) named her Woman of the Year for 2016 and she was awarded an MBE in 2017 for 'Services to Digital Technology and Tech Development' and in 2018 Women in IT named her Diversity Leader of the Year. More recently, WeAreTechWomen awarded Debbie their Editor's Choice Award for 2020 and Computer Weekly named her Most Influential Woman in UK IT for 2019. Debbie serves on the Institute of Coding's Diversity Board and on the government's Digital Economy Council and its Money and Pensions Service advisory board.

Erica Gibson is an anthropologist working in technology, and currently the Global Head of User Research for SumUp in Berlin, Germany. She previously worked as a professor of Anthropology and Women's and Gender Studies, teaching and conducting research on cultural aspects of pregnancy and birth in Mexico, the US, and Italy. After transitioning to the tech world she has worked internationally in healthcare, telecommunications, media, and financial services. Her passion is bringing together people from all walks of life to create an inclusive space in technology. She is also a founding partner of Before You Code, a consultancy dedicated to helping companies focus on their prospective users so that they make the best possible decisions before they start building their products.

Dr. Leda Glyptis is Chief Client Officer of 10x Banking and focuses on driving client success for existing and new 10x clients. Leda is a former banker, technology executive, and founding CEO of 11:FS Foundry, where she led the growth of its modular core digital banking offering. Prior to that, Leda was Chief Innovation Officer at Qatar National Bank, the largest bank in the Middle East and North Africa, with responsibilities for employee-driven and market-led innovation strategy and execution. Before QNB, Leda was a Director at business and technology consulting firm Sapient, focusing on digital transformation and emerging technologies, and led EMEA innovation at BNY Mellon. Leda joined BNY Mellon from FinTech start-up Great East London Software, where she served as head of services development. Leda holds an M.A. from King's College, Cambridge, and an M.Sc.

and Ph.D. from the London School of Economics and Political Science. She has taught politics, global governance, and management principles, whilst working in management roles across various industries.

Kenzy Goodwin is a Partner at Finceler8, a FinTech sales organisation with a mission to source best in breed FinTech firms and accelerate their commercial engagement process with financial institutions. It has a dedicated sales team with over 200 years of collective experience in sales and business development in financial markets. Prior to Finceler8, Kenzy spent twenty years at BlackRock as a senior equity trader where she traded all equity investment products: quant, fundamental active equity and index funds. Kenzy is passionate about FinTech, innovation, and inclusivity. She believes diversity of thought is essential for growth and successful idea generation. She enjoys her roles as a mentor at Level 39—a community of leaders in FinTech and as a mentor for the Cherie Blair Mentoring Programme—supporting women entrepreneurs around the world. Kenzy also co-Chaired a personal development programme for two years whilst at BlackRock and she is fluent in English and Arabic.

Emmy Granström is a marketing professional with a background in financial services technology and regulatory compliance. Her area of expertise is on building scalable marketing programmes that deliver the combination of short-term results and long-term value that scaling B2B organisations require. Emmy is currently leading the strategic marketing efforts at SteelEye, a UK-based RegTech scale-up on a mission to help establish and maintain trust in the financial markets by making it easy for clients to accurately comply with financial regulation. Prior to SteelEye, Emmy was the Co-Head of Marketing and Corporate Communications at Cinnober (acquired by Nasdaq in January 2019), responsible for the marketing and corporate communications of two Group subsidiaries, and co-responsible for the Group. Working in FinTech, which combines two industries that are traditionally very male, Emmy is a keen advocate for diversity and inclusion and passionate about how we can attract and celebrate female talent.

Sophie Guibard is the Chief Growth Officer at OpenPayd, responsible for revenue growth and leading Marketing, Sales, Customer Success, and Corporate Development teams. She has spent the last 10+ years developing and executing the go-to market strategy for Banking-as-a-Service (BaaS) and Embedded Finance propositions across Europe. OpenPayd is a leading global payments and banking-as-a-service platform for the digital economy. Through its API-driven technology, businesses can embed financial services into their products and create the seamless user experiences needed to drive business growth.

Monica Gupta is an experienced FinTech and banking professional with a demonstrated history of working in the financial services industry (M&A, Corporate banking, SME, FinTech lending, and Payments). Skilled in Credit Analysis, Equities, Capital Markets, Mergers and Acquisitions, Financial Modelling, payment, and lending solutions. Strong finance professional with an M.B.A. focused in Finance from Xavier Institute of Management and CFA level 2.

Nim Haas has been working in marketing and the technology sector for over 20 years. Having grown up and lived in various countries from France, Australia, Singapore, Monaco, America, UK, and now Spain, she is a true melting pot of culture, and has frequently used this to her advantage in understanding cross-cultural differences, and how this impacts business decisions especially when defining marketing and communication strategies across borders. Within the first year of launching her agency, TechFuse was awarded 'Best B2B Specialist Marketing Agency of the Year'—UK, in the FinTech Awards 2021 category by Wealth and International Finance. Prior to founding her B2B marketing agency, Nim provided marketing and communication consultancy for numerous companies in FinTech, PayTech, and RegTech sectors. She also led the global marketing for Global Processing Services, the issuer processor behind FinTech disruptors such as Revolut, Starling Bank, Xinja, Curve, Soldo, Pleo, and Anna Money. Her dedication to her role and the sector she works in can be seen through her involvement in various initiatives she undertakes. She is a business mentor at Barclay Rise, Global Exco Board Member at Global FinTech Impact Forum, Founding member of b-yond.co, Founder of The Payments Clinic, Advisory Board member for CCGroup PR, Advisory Board member for Women in Tech, Global Movement, and Advisory Board Member at Emerging FinTech Forum. She has been recognised by the Holmes Report amongst the top 25 Innovators in Marketing & Communication for EMEA—2018, and by Innovate Finance as Standout 35, Women in FinTech 2019, and Women in FinTech Powerlist 2020, as well as finalist for the awards of 'Tech Leader of the Year 2019' by the UK Inclusion Board.

Alison Harwood heads the London branch of Hamburg-based Varengold Bank, a leading financier of European FinTechs, and is responsible for developing its FinTech lending business across Western Europe. Widely connected within the European FinTech ecosystem and the market for FinTech financing, she is always on the lookout for bold and innovative new clients with customer-centric products or services that add significant value. Alison is an expert on the nuts and bolts of setting up and maintaining successful bank–FinTech financing relationships and a regular speaker on podcasts and at industry events. Prior to joining Varengold in 2015, Alison worked in structured finance at Barclays Capital and as a tax/financial services regulation lawyer with Linklaters.

Lucy Heavens currently leads marketing at Wealth Dynamix has 20+ years experience in FinTech. Previously, Lucy held senior marketing positions at global technology firms (Fiserv, SimCorp and IBM) and high-growth scale-up firms (Equipos, Qumram, and CUBE), where she was instrumental in growing visibility and bridging the gap between marketing and sales to help achieve revenue targets. Her marketing expertise ranges from product and partner marketing through to digital marketing, lead generation and communications. Lucy is a self-confessed tech-geek, recognised globally for her thought leadership and expertise spanning FinTech, RegTech, WealthTech, Big Data, and Digital Transformation. An exceptional communicator and public commentator, Lucy has earned her place as an industry influencer, regularly featuring in the Planet Compliance Top 50 RegTech Influencers list, a Top 10 Expert on the Onalytica 100 RegTech Influencers list and has appeared in the Innovate Finance Women in FinTech Powerlist in 2017, 2019, and 2020. As a Co-Founder of the not-for-profit association RegTech Women, Lucy is extremely passionate about diversity and inclusion and actively involved in supporting and promoting the vital role women play in driving RegTech success.

Jamie Howard is the Chief Technology Officer at Capital On Tap, a leading UK FinTech firm for SME lending and payments. Capital on Tap offer SMEs in the UK, Spain, and the US a credit facility up to £100,000, a Corporate Visa card and payment services to help grow their business. As of July 2021, Capital on Tap has lent over £3 Billion and have been named one of the 50 fastest-growing tech companies in the UK by the Sunday Times. Having worked in the technology industry for over 20 years, Jamie is acutely aware of the benefits of growing and fostering a diverse and inclusive team and is a fervent proponent of attracting talent from all backgrounds, including but not limited to women, people of colour, and members of the LGBTQIA+ community.

Caroline Hughes is Chief Executive Officer and Co-Founder of Lifetise, a FinTech company that helps people plan how to afford big life decisions, like buying a home or starting a family. Caroline has been named as a standout rising star and a senior leader of FinTech by Innovate Finance on its annual Women in FinTech Powerlist. She is passionate about building feminist FinTech. Lifetise was one of the companies selected for Accenture's prestigious FinTech accelerator programme in 2019 and the Mayor of London's Business Growth Programme in 2021.

Ritesh Jain is an Entrepreneurial Technology Leader, Board Advisor, start-up Founder, and a Ph.D. in Payments Innovation, Open Banking, and Open Finance. Over the last 20 years, Ritesh has been at the forefront of the payments industry, leading the future of VISA payments and introducing Apple Pay in Europe/UK. He has led the transformation across many global organisations. Ritesh's vast experience and expertise in the payments industry is now seeing him play crucial advisory roles to many organisations, such as the G20 Initiative for Financial Inclusion (Member); Open Banking in EU and Africa; Harvard Business Review; payment regulators and government bodies for their initiative in social and financial inclusion; MIT Global in Tech Panel (Member). He has also been a mentor to the UK Parliament Digital initiative and many other start-ups. Ritesh is also an advisor and visiting lecturer to leading business schools and universities globally, apart from being a regular speaker and author and a strong advocate of diversity and inclusion. After leaving HSBC as Chief Operating Officer Digital, Ritesh co-founded Infynit, harnessing his knowledge of and penchant for digital payments.

Rahma Javed is the Director of Engineering for the restaurants group at Deliveroo. She focuses on helping Deliveroo become the preferred partner for its restaurants and driving growth and profitability for them. Prior to this, Rahma was a senior engineering leader at Wealthfront where she led the financial services area that focused on building products in the financial advisory space like the 529 College Savings Plan as well as the Portfolio Line of Credit. Originally from Toronto, Canada where she did her schooling from the University of Toronto in Computer Engineering. Along with working at start-ups and mid-sized companies, Rahma has worked at larger corporations like Microsoft (wherein she was working in the Windows and then Bing team) as well as IBM Canada and Blackberry.

Lindsey Jayne has held product leadership roles in all sorts of organisations, from charities to global corporations. In government she co-led GOV.UK at the world-leading Government Digital Service, before heading to Farfetch, a global tech company that was preparing to list on the stock exchange. More recently she found a home in FinTech, and was the Vice President of Product at Monzo, leading all of product through a rocket ship ride of growth from 1 million to 3 million users, and a quadrupling of the company. Today she leads Product at Yoco, a rapidly growing African making it simple for small businesses to get paid and manage their money. She is an advisor to start-ups starting and scaling their product teams and is known for working on products that challenge incumbents or the status quo. She is a fan of simplicity, inclusivity, and dresses with pockets.

Michelle Johnson became Head of the UK and Ireland team at Fexco Payments & FX one week before the UK entered its first COVID lockdown, catapulting her into a situation with rapid requirement to bring to bear her agile and flexible management approach. A strategic thinker, Michelle excels at asking why we do what we do, questioning preconceptions, and hitting challenging targets. She believes that innovative solutions are unveiled by motivated teams who are empowered to challenge the status quo. Michelle takes great pride in developing her team of industry experts and entrusting them to surpass expectations. Michelle has extensive experience delivering finance and technology initiatives, starting her career in North America, joining Fexco in their Middle East and Africa office, before moving to the UK where she now resides. Michelle is a certified Project Management Professional® and earned her M.B.A. in Strategic Planning from Herriot-Watt University in 2019.

Seema Khinda Johnson is Co-Founder and Chief Operating Officer at Nuggets, an award-winning, enterprise-grade, consumer-ready decentralised, digital identity and payment platform, that helps organisations to protect customer data and create trust in transactions whilst giving customers a frictionless, seamless experience. Nuggets is the only platform of its kind that truly brings together payments and ID, utilising self-sovereign data principles. Seema has received widespread recognition across the industry, having recently won Deutsche Bank's Female FinTech Competition, Women in Payments' Unicorn Challenge, was awarded the Booking.com Technology Playmaker Entrepreneur of the Year and also listed as one of the Most Influential Women in Payments, by PaymentsSource.

Before founding Nuggets, Seema spent more than 20 years leading teams and delivering large-scale commercialisation, products, campaigns, and projects with brands like Skype and Microsoft.

Jonas Karles is the Chief Operating Officer and Co-Founder of Minna Technologies with 12+ years of experience in people leadership. He has scaled business from 3 people to 85+ talents all over the world with a strong focus on operational excellence and successful company cultures. Minna Technologies is a Swedish tech company established in 2016, on a mission to help retail banks deliver powerful digital experiences within subscription management. Partnering with top-tier banks across Europe and backed by some of the biggest financial companies in the world, millions of people benefit from Minna's subscription solutions.

Samantha Knights has a passion for using technology to solve problems for people. She was encouraged by her parents but only discovered Computer Science at university in South Africa. In London she built her career in financial services institutions, from working as a trading desk developer at an investment bank, software engineer at a hedge fund to leading teams in trading and an asset manager. Being head of architecture has enabled her to remain in the technical detail but with the mandate to bring about change, also set an example to other women that it is possible to be in a technical leadership position. She is driven to improve diversity in the workplace, from hiring to supporting return to work for mothers, becoming one herself recently. She is sick of the fact that she went from being one of the few women in the classroom to the few in the boardroom!

Serena Koivurinta is known for 'getting it done' whatever the situation requires, and she does this by actively speaking to customers and understanding the root cause of the opportunity. Skilled in product development Serena brings in views from across marketing, sales, engineering, finance, and design to deliver complex, technology products with a customer-first mindset. Her no-nonsense attitude combined with experience leading international development teams allows her to take a diverse perspective whilst balancing risk versus reward before 'getting it done'.

Jenny Kong is the Global Head of Marketing at Wirex, a leading payments platform aiming to make digital currencies more accessible in the everyday. Over eight years specialised in social media and digital marketing, her experience spans across award-winning advertising agencies and media agencies in the Asia-Pacific. She's spent the last few years in Europe, immersed in FinTech and digital currencies with Wirex. The UK-based firm developed the world's first contactless payment card that gives users the ability to seamlessly spend crypto and traditional currencies in real life. She is an avid advocate for female representation in the tech industries and has launched the inaugural 'Rising Women In Crypto Power List', celebrating and raising awareness in the sector. At Wirex, she currently leads an all-female social media and consumer marketing team.

Nicky Koopman is a Dutch business executive serving as the Senior Vice President Partnerships of AEVI. She is a pioneer in digital innovation with over 15 years' experience working in Broadcast Media, Venture Capital, and FinTech across the globe, with expertise in developing and expanding businesses with digital at the heart. Nicky uses her entrepreneurial spirit and openness as well as her positive attitude to encourage others to go the extra mile and grow to their full potential.

AEVI provides merchant-facing businesses—banks, acquirers, PSPs, ISOs, ISVs, and others—with a platform that enables merchants to run their business smarter by giving them easy access to any payment technology and business solution for the best in-store customer experience. AEVI's cloud-based platform empowers them to upgrade to more agile and data-driven propositions, driving greater efficiency, more innovation, and an improved customer journey across all channels.

Valentina Kristensen is the Director of Growth & Communications at OakNorth. She began working with its Co-Founders, Rishi Khosla and Joel Perlman, consultancy-side in June 2015, and joined full-time in 2016, helping to build the brand and community. She is a passionate advocate for improving the female talent pipeline in FinTech and financial services, sitting on the Steering Committee for FinTECHTalents, and being ElevatHer's first ambassador for the UK. In 2018, Valentina participated in the Money 20/20 Europe Payments Race where she travelled from Istanbul to Amsterdam using only wearable payments technology—no cash or cards. In 2019, she participated in the round the world race where she only used cash, travelling across 13 countries in 12 days.

Regina Lau is a global strategy and financial leader driven by a passion to help brands grow and scale. With 20+ years of experience in payments and FinTech, she has worked at both public and private equity-backed companies to leverage the enormous growth opportunities in international expansion, ecommerce, and digitization of financial services. As a strong supporter of diversity and inclusion and financial inclusion, Regina has been executive sponsor of many diversity and inclusion initiatives, including creating "Women in Management" programmes to increase leadership training and mentoring. She has also actively led recruitment, employee engagement, and development programmes to ensure that work environments are balanced for gender, culture, lifestyle, and professional backgrounds. Regina currently sits on several boards, including European Women Payments Network (EWPN) and also Dali Spaces & InvestFem, a global community that empowers, enables, and provides female founders access to investors and resources for success.

Alice Leguay is a Director at Clim8 Invest, a FinTech for sustainable investments. Prior to Clim8, Alice was a Partner at HUBX, a capital markets FinTech backed by Barclays and LSEG. She founded Emolument, a salary data platform which focused on highlighting the gender pay gap. Alice started her career at Morgan Stanley in HY & Distressed sales & trading. Passionate about empowering women as leaders, Alice is NED and Mentor for Athena40 and Global Thinkers Forum, and for the Like Minded Female network. She is an alumni of the Cambridge Institute for Sustainability Leadership and holds an M.A. in Modern History from Oxford University.

Johanna Maria Leiner is a strong advocate for Diversity & Inclusion and has organised several networking events and panal discussions for women in the finance and the FinTech industry. She is an official Ambassador for the European Women in Payment Network (EWPN) and the FinTech Ladies, two networking groups supporting women in business. In 2019, Johanna received the EWPN Award 'Positive Troublemaker' for her work in gender equality and ethics. After obtaining her law degree from the University of Innsbruck (Austria) and studying at UCD School of Law in Dublin (Ireland), Johanna worked for Financial Market Authorities in Liechtenstein and Austria. Today her role is Vice President Compliance Governance & Ethics at Paysafe where she is responsible for Compliance Training, Policy, Assurance, Compliance Risk Assessments, and Conduct and Ethics. Johanna serves as a member of the Global Practitioner Advisory Board for the International Compliance Association (ICA).

Roisin Levine has been named in the Women in FinTech Powerlist for three years running and has held senior positions at a number of well-known high-growth tech scale-ups including; uSwitch, Zoopla, and now Wise (formerly known as TransferWise). Roisin was recently nominated for the Women in Finance 'Young Leader of the Year' award for her contributions as Head of Banks at the award-winning FinTech Flux. She has provided articles and commentary on FinTech innovation and trends for publications such as Sifted, Forbes, and Techcrunch. As a FinTech public speaker she has featured regularly as a panellist and interviewee for events and podcasts, including 11:FS's FinTech Insider, Barclays Bank, Cass Business School, Deloitte, Women of FinTech, Bottomline Technologies, London School of Banking and Finance, TechNation, Business Banking Forum, and FinTech Alliance.

Kimberley Lewis is Head of Active Ownership at Schroders, a global asset manager. In her role, Kimberley and her team are actively influencing corporate behaviour to ensure that the companies Schroders invests in are managed in a sustainable way. Previously Kimberley was Director of Engagement for Federated Hermes International and Senior Director of Social Investment at Pfizer Inc., where she led a team that was responsible for the strategy and implementation of the company's ex-US corporate responsibility work.

Evgenia Loginova wears multiple hats within BPC, a leading payment solution company headquartered in Switzerland. She is Senior Vice President, Chief Strategy Officer at BPC, and Founder and Chief Executive Officer at Radar Payments. She has been working for BPC for over six years and has global responsibility for corporate strategy, marketing, and business growth. She is successfully leading the development of BPC through the rapidly changing landscape of payments, banking, commerce, and mobility. Since joining BPC, Evgenia has spearheaded the creation of new ventures that positively impact BPC's growth, with the forecast to double the company's revenue by 2023. She founded Radar Payments, a paytech which translates the group's SaaS transformation programme and its vision for next-generation cloud-based payments. Radar Payments offers white-label payment processing services to banks, PSPs, and FinTechs. BPC's newest and most ambitious paytech is expected to generate the major part of its revenues over the next few years. Before joining BPC, Evgenia held executive director roles at Goldman Sachs. She studied management at the London School of Economics and is based in London.

Gabriel MacSweeney started her career organising large-scale technology events like London Tech Week, and made the move into FinTech in 2018. Whilst at Fluidly, an AI-powered tool that helps small businesses manage their cashflow, she was promoted to lead the Account Management function, after proving her commercial acumen. She now leads on Commercial Strategy and Strategic Partnerships at Codat, a high-growth scale-up company that helps FinTechs and financial institutions seamlessly connect to their business customers' financial software. In her spare time, she enjoys performing and keeping fit.

Rita Martins is the FinTech Partnerships Lead, for Finance and Risk, at HSBC. Building and managing relationships with high-potential start-ups and driving collaboration between FinTechs and traditional financial services. Rita worked previously at Ernst and Young and Accenture, advising C-Suite on the applicability of RPA and AI tools in finance and driving large-scale transformation projects, gaining deep insight on best practices across the industry. A recognised FinTech expert, Rita was recognised in the TOP 30 Women in FinTech by Rework and Women in FinTech Powerlist 2020 by Innovate Finance. She is a regular speaker at financial industry events panels and a judge at FinTech innovation awards. Rita actively partners with a number of mentoring programmes and communities to share her knowledge and help realise transformational ideas to drive change. She is currently mentoring at Startupbootcamp sustainability and is an advocate at Tech London Advocates (TLA).

Emmanuelle Mathey works for Schroders plc where she is the Group Head of Credit Risk as well as the co-Chief Risk Officer of the Wealth Management entities. She spent the previous 10 years working at JP Morgan in London and Sydney where she was an Executive Director managing Credit Risk for the Investment Bank. Her focus was predominantly in the Asset Management space (including Hedge Funds, Private Equity, Real Estate, and Pension funds). Emmanuelle also chairs SchOUT, Schroders' LGBT+ employee network. Outside of her day job, Emmanuelle is very actively involved in Corporate Responsibility both with philanthropic initiatives and Diversity and Inclusion efforts, focusing specifically on LGBT+, women, and social mobility. She is a financial advisor to the Cripplegate Foundation in Islington and a Non-Executive Director for Moneyline, a sustainable social enterprise focused on being a fair finance provider. Emmanuelle holds a Master's in International Public Law from Université Paul Cezanne in France and Tübingen Universität in Germany.

Lauren McEwan is an all-round data nerd, originally from Australia and now based in London. She believes information is an asset worthy of careful curation and protection, but that it's there to be used and shared for everyone's benefit. Lauren's early career was in information and records management, and she has since made the jump to information security. This gives her a big picture view of managing information securely and effectively throughout its whole lifecycle.

Monica Millares is a dynamic FinTech entrepreneur passionate about delivering solutions that create change in people's financial lives. Her expertise is product development, customer experience, and bringing the best out of people to create high-performance teams. Monica joined BigPay with the vision to build the first South East Asian challenger bank: to make financial services accessible to everyone, and put customer needs at the core of the solutions. Prior to BigPay, she started her FinTech journey in Tandem Bank. Her experience in retail and development banks, payment schemes, corporate and start-up environments, as well as in Latin America, Europe, and Asia, has allowed Monica to develop a diverse and unique perspective and style. She holds a Master's degree in Information Systems from the London School of Economics and has a background in Industrial Engineering. Monica is the creator and host of Celebrate You!—the personal development, career growth, entrepreneurship, and money podcast for millennial women.

Adrienne Muir is the Chief Operating Officer at VoxSmart, a leading communications surveillance technology provider. She has over 20 years' market experience working for Exchanges and Financial Technology providers with an emphasis on Markets Infrastructure, Business operations, Technical Delivery, and People Management. Adrienne has held a number of senior positions globally at LIFFE, New Zealand Exchange (NZX), Trayport Ltd., and the London Stock Exchange. Adrienne has a passion for women in business and believes that natural instincts and aptitude are not tapped into enough when it comes to promoting women in the workplace. She leads from the front and often found mentoring at work or after hours helping share her experiences with others. VoxSmart is a SaaS surveillance technology provider that designs, develops, and deploys software to better manage business risk and meet regulatory requirements.

Sangeetha Narasimhan is currently the Global Acquisition Marketing Director at Mambu where she leads the growth marketing for the regions across the globe. Having worked for global companies such as Hewlett Packard Enterprise, Sage, Ingenico, and then Worldline as well as start-ups, Sangeetha brings a wealth of experience in helping businesses sharpen their growth strategies with marketing. Sangeetha has a Bachelor of Science degree in Visual Communication from Loyola College, India, as well as a Master's in International Business and Management from Sheffield Hallam University in the UK. She is passionate about gender diversity and inclusiveness, building high-performing teams, and bringing authenticity to marketing. In her free time she enjoys hiking, reading, watching films, and following cricket.

Lax Narayan currently works as an Application Support Manager at TD Securities. Lax has over 12 years' experience in Technology within the Financial Services Industry. She graduated from Queen Mary University with a Master's in Computing and Information Systems in 2008. She started her career at LCH as a graduate in 2009 working in various roles within Technology including Software Development, System Analysis, Testing and Production Support. She is an advocate for diversity and inclusion. She co-leads Women in Tech initiatives that promote diversity and make STEM roles more accessible to women. Outside of work she is actively mentoring university students encouraging more young women to choose technology careers within the financial services sector.

Zoe Newman is the US Managing Director of Capital on Tap. Since joining the company right at the very beginning she has led operations, partnerships, and co-branded card programmes and recently launched the business into Spain and now the US.

Helena Nordegren is a Sales Executive at Finastra, one of the world's largest FinTech's, with more than 9,000 clients, including 90 of the top 100 banks globally. Finastra has the scale and reach that builds long-lasting relationships and puts customers and their customers' first. After a start in the Ministry for Foreign Affairs and the Swedish Prime Minister's Office, she was hired by financial institution Alfred Berg that when acquired by ABN AMRO, which brought her into banking. She had the pleasure to work for Fortis Bank/BNP Paribas, Deutsche Bank, and JP Morgan before she entered the IT world at Tieto and from there to Finastra. She's an experienced sales and relationship manager in complex sales with a passion for making customers successful, a curiosity for technology, and an entrepreneurial mindset. Her goal is to act and cooperate in an inclusive way with passion, compassion, curiosity, and humour.

Claire Norman has over 7 years of experience in counter financial crime, specialising in fraud prevention, and has worked her way up from an analyst to Head of Financial Crime across a range of industries. She has also completed a Master's degree in Counter Fraud & Counter Corruption Studies with the University of Portsmouth, and is currently doing her part-time Ph.D.—focusing on the role of insider fraud within business. As someone who stammers, Claire has also faced and prevailed over many challenges in education and the workplace. She also set up her own voluntary initiative by the name of 'STUC' (Stammerers Through University Consultancy) in 2014, whereby she hosts events at collaborating universities all over the UK to improve the experience for their students and staff who stammer. She runs this single-handed, alongside her Ph.D. and her full-time job. As well as campaigning for invisible disability awareness, Claire actively drives for the removal of stigma surrounding mental health in the workplace.

Elena Betés Novoa is an international lead focusing on increasing the RVu presence in Europe and scaling our operations globally. She is inspired to bring more transparency to all markets in order to empower the world to make better decisions, whilst levelling the playing field for all. Elena joined RVu through the acquisition of Penguin Portals, where she held the position of Chief Executive Officer. As a serial entrepreneur specialised in launching comparison platforms, with successes and failures that have made her very resilient over the years, Elena maintains an unwavering ambition to replicate the success achieved in the UK, Spain, and France in more parts of Europe and beyond. She holds an M.B.A. from IESE. Spanish, born in Canada and married to a German, Elena considers herself a citizen of the world, a world that she aims to improve. Elena lives in Madrid with her husband, two kids and their growing team of animals—a dog, a horse, and a little fish on the way!

Eimear O'Connor is the Chief Operating Officer and a founding member of the management team at Form3, with responsibility for all aspects of business and service operations. Eimear has worked and consulted within financial services organisations on strategy, product, and operations for over 15 years. She joined Form3 from Barclays where she was Retail and Commercial Director for Pingit, the award-winning open market payments platform and has held strategy and consulting roles at Visa, BearingPoint, and Capco. Eimear holds a BSc Finance from University College Cork and an MBS Strategic Management and Planning from the Smurfit Graduate School of Business, University College Dublin.

Louise O'Shea is Chief Executive Officer of Confused.com, and she is passionate about empowering customers to make better buying decisions and providing services that enable personalised financial journeys. Under her leadership, the company has been returned to its former start-up culture, by focusing on optimising the company's core InsurTech function. Louise joined Confused.com in 2016, firstly as Business Development Manager and then Finance Director, before taking on the role as CEO. Passionate about disrupting industry stereotypes, Louise uses her platform to actively drive FinTech across Wales through her positions on the InsurTech 2.0 and FinTech Wales boards. In her spare time, Louise enjoys spending time with her two young daughters and husband in the Welsh countryside. She is a keen swimmer and plays the piano whenever she has the opportunity, but her favourite pastime is to play chess—as strategy is never too far from her mind! After reading History at Edinburgh University, Louise trained as a Chartered Accountant and soon realised her love for technology and business, holding positions at PwC and Fujitsu, before joining the Admiral Group.

Miia Paavola is a Product Manager at Pleo, focusing on admin and book-keeping experience, innovating and challenging the status quo of current solutions in spending. With multiple years of experience in FinTech, from an established innovative bank, start-ups, and software, she has gone through a change from partnership- and customer-facing roles to a full product role in a FinTech unicorn. Miia is also the Founder of Product Feast, connecting product professionals through great food and hosting a podcast where she takes these talented product people to dinners and discusses the learnings and lessons they've gone through in their careers.

Diana Paredes is the Chief Executive Officer and Co-Founder of Suade, a software platform that enables financial institutions to understand and deliver their regulatory requirements. Prior to founding Suade, Diana had a successful career in investment banking, covering all asset classes at Barclays and Merrill Lynch, across sales, trading and structuring. Whilst working in the industry, she saw an opportunity to innovate and launch her current FinTech/RegTech start-up. She believes that a data-driven approach to regulation is the key to preventing the next financial crisis.

Irene Perdomo is Managing Director and Head of Product Strategy at Gresham Investment Management. Prior to joining Gresham, Irene was CEO and Managing Partner of Devet Capital, a boutique commodities-focused quant firm. Prior to co-founding Devet, she traded base metals at Noble Resources in Singapore and, before that, she was co-responsible for commodities product development in the Commodity Investor Structuring team at Barclays in London. She is the co-author of *Pricing and Hedging Financial*

Derivatives: A Guide for Practitioners (Wiley, 2013), and has been a guest lecturer in Mathematics and Finance at Queen Mary University and at Imperial College London. Irene holds an M.B.A. from IESE Barcelona, a degree in Computer Science Engineering from her home university in Uruguay, and studied finance at the University of Chicago Booth School of Business.

Rashmi Prabhakar is an experienced FinTech professional with 20+ years of experience in driving Strategic Change and Technology Transformation initiatives within Banking, Energy, and FinTech industries. She is currently Chief of Staff—Professional Services at Finastra driving strategic transformation programmes, engagement, and communications, prior to which she ran European Regional Operations. Rashmi has a Bachelor's in Computer Science Engineering and has a proven track record in rolling out Change Programmes with a focus on Account Strategy, Customer Engagement, and Business Growth, thereby boosting Customer Engagement and Success.

Additionally, she is hugely passionate about creating an environment which fosters equality, diversity, and inclusive behaviour and empowering men and women by rolling out Unconscious Bias, Mentoring, Menopause, Mental Health awareness, and Male Advocacy Programs. She lives in London with her husband and children, aged 13 and 7, who keep her grounded and ensure she appreciates the simple pleasures in life!

Hannah Lana Preston has a purpose that is to 'connect with people passionate about making a difference'. Her mission is to collaborate with organisations to discover and deliver technology that drives business value. Hannah's career began in lending, underwriting, and development finance, which gave her a great foundation. She saw enormous benefits in digital banking, and enjoyed being part of the transformation. Hannah devotes herself to inspiring and guiding organisations to meet the needs of their customers in the digital age. Working at some of the world's leading software houses and start-ups including CA Technologies, Mulesoft, FeatureSpace, and Minna Tech. Experience has taught her about the interconnections of Digital Identity, AI, Security, API management, and personal finance management. Hannah's work helping the Banking industry to meet EBA's SCA guidelines, won her widespread recognition as one of Innovate Finance's 'Most Powerful Women in FinTech in 2017'. Since then she has played an instrumental role in showcasing the value of API-led business strategies to banks, helping many organisations create a more connected financial ecosystem and embrace the concepts of open banking.

Payal Raina is a Founder of FinTech Marketing community. She is a pioneer in founding the very first B2B FinTech Marketing community which is built for and by FinTech marketers breaking the silos between Financial Services firms and Technology providers. She is also Global Head of Marketing at Torstone Technology, a leading FinTech company, provider of cloud-based post-trade technology to financial institutions. In her role, Payal oversees planning, development, and execution of Torstone's marketing, PR, and branding initiatives—across global markets—in UK and Europe, Nordics, Asia, and North America. Payal has been in the financial technology industry since 2004. With over two decades of experience in B2B marketing for global financial and technology companies (Microsoft, General Electric, Barclays) in Europe and North America, Payal has a wealth of experience implementing successful marketing strategies.

Kelly Read-Parish is the Chief Operating Officer of Credit Kudos, an FCA-authorised credit bureau and Open Banking provider that uses detailed financial data to enable better credit decisions. Kelly has deep experience in finance and technology across credit risk, portfolio management, strategy, and operations. She is passionate about using technology to make finance fairer and easier for everyone. Before joining Credit Kudos, Kelly worked on the investment team of venture capital fund Pi Labs, where she sourced and executed seed and series A deals. Kelly had a hands-on role working with portfolio companies, advising on finance, hiring, and operations. Prior to that, Kelly was part of the fixed income portfolio management team of Prudential Financial/PGIM, an asset management firm with over $1 trillion in AUM. Kelly worked in both London and in the US, evaluating risk and pricing for portfolios of corporate and government debt. Kelly began her career with financial data provider FactSet (NYSE: FDS), advising large banks on the use of complex financial data products and services. Kelly holds an MBA from London Business School and a BA(Hons) in Politics and History from the University of Exeter.

Laura Rofe has a wealth of experience within the Finance and Payments sectors spanning 12 years in both the Australian and UK markets. She specialises in people management, partnerships, and account management, and takes on responsibility for strategic growth and overall portfolio management. Continuing education is really important to Laura and in line with her commitment to professional and personal success, she has just completed her Executive M.B.A. and also has a bachelor's degree in International Business and Marketing. Laura is very passionate about giving back to others and dedicating time to educating, celebrating the wins and impacting change when it comes to gender equality, across all walks of her life. She is an advocate for female empowerment and supports this through a number of initiatives and programmes like mentoring young women. Further to this, Laura has also been appointed as an Associate Trustee on the Women's Advisory Board for UK Charity, IARS. On a personal note, Laura is always up for a challenge, looking for the next thing to set her mind to and is well known for her enthusiastic and positive zest for life!

Karen Rudich Chief Executive Officer and Co-Founder of ELEMENTARYb has nearly 20 years' experience in business. She is known for identifying opportunities to grow revenues and boost efficiencies, and has a successful track record in assembling effective teams and putting in place structures and systems to generate bottom-line P&L impact. She has led large-scale transformation programmes at UBS, BNP Paribas, Barclays, and Lloyds. Most recently she was Founder/CEO of a challenger firm focusing on speedy P&L-driving transformations and technology integration for top-tier banks and cutting-edge FinTech firms.

Iraide Ruiz is a Telecoms Engineer from the Basque Country, in Northern Spain. She has worked in different industries since graduating: embedded, research, gaming, and banking. She started her career as a C developer and moved to web development and Java some years later. A couple of years back she transitioned from a senior engineer role to an engineering manager role. Her personal experience as a woman in technology has made her become an advocate for diversity and inclusion. She created the first women in technology circle in one of the companies she worked for and she's been involved with several women in tech forums in London. She currently works for IG Group in the city of London, where, apart from managing teams of backend developers, she is the Inclusion and Diversity Champion for technology. This role has given her the opportunity to lead a group of highly committed individuals to deliver several initiatives to help improve gender balance and inclusion in the tech department.

Liza Russell has over 18 years' experience in financial services and consulting. Managing high-scale customer-centric operations and leading change and remediation projects in global retail and wealth management banks. As a senior leader and mentor who has managed hundreds of individuals, her knowledge and appreciation of a diverse and inclusive workforce has been instrumental in her success. Three years ago, Liza decided to leave the corporate world to join a FinTech start-up, Inbotiqa, where she could bring her extensive experience and skills to support and build a culture for diversity, equality, and inclusion within the expanding team. The focus starts at the hiring process, ensuring there is a mix of qualified individual applicants joining the team where they are encouraged to share their suggestions and opinions to contribute to the team's success. Each individual is valued and respected and that is what drives and sustains a strong team culture.

Dr. Louise Ryan is the Head of Portfolio Management for Close Brothers Merchant Bank. She has been working within the finance industry as part of the Technology team for Close Brothers Merchant Bank since 2016. Louise is an advocate for women in technology and believes in helping others as much as they have helped her! She is currently the coordinator for the technology graduate scheme within Close Brothers and has been keenly involved in women in FinTech events hosted and attended by Close Brothers.

Jenny Sadler is an International Talent Acquisition leader with extensive track record with in-house and agency positions. Experienced in management and strategy as well as implementation of two recruitment systems. She has delivered recruitment drives globally. She has strong experience in vendor management, direct attraction methods, competency-based interviewing, e-recruitment and testing; as well as employer branding, digital strategy, and delivering high-profile recruitment campaigns. She is also experienced in delivering innovative strategies to promote accountability and awareness around diversity and inclusion.

Patricia Salume a second-time FinTech founder, is the Co-Founder and Chief Operating Officer of vHelp; a leading provider of SaaS tools for the third and public sectors. vHelp was born during the first COVID-19 lockdown to solve a real issue faced by charities and organisations managing volunteers. Patricia and the team secured private and public investment to build vHelp. The company is now growing and developing a suite of digital products to allow their customers to embrace digital and become more efficient.

Patricia started her career in Marketing in her native Brazil. She then spent 10 years in the third/public sectors as a business development manager. After gaining an M.B.A. at Henley Business School in 2012 and having her first child, Patricia left her full-time job and became a management consultant working with large corporates as well as SMEs and start-ups before starting her entrepreneurship journey in 2016.

Roxane Sanguinetti is Head of Fixed Income and Investor Relations at GHCO, one of the fastest-growing liquidity providers specialising in ETFs. Passionate about technology and entrepreneurship, she joined GHCO just as the company emerged as a leading FinTech business, to advance the fixed income trading. She also leads the company's PR and fundraising efforts. Prior to joining GHCO, she held positions at Merrill Lynch and the capital markets FinTech HUBX. Fierce advocate for diversity and inclusion, Roxane started mentoring early-stage founders. She joined Alma Angels from its early days in 2019, an inclusive community of angel investors who are passionate about actively investing in and supporting ambitious female founders building companies with global scale.

Billie Simmons (she/her) is the Co-Founder and Chief Operating Officer of Daylight. Previously, she founded a start-up to help trans and non-binary people access safe services. Her background is in marketing and software engineering at FinTech focused companies such as Techstars and Anthemis group. She regularly speaks on LGBT+ initiatives in mental health and technology and has spoken at, amongst others, Google, WeWork, and Money2020.

Arshi Singh is a Product Leader passionate about solving customer problems with an engineer's focus and a general manager's view. Her other passion is raising her daughter to become a confident and well-rounded woman. Arshi's goal is to create awesome products and inspire other product managers to achieve their best. She has 18 years of experience across technology and finance. Arshi has been the Head of NA Product at ComplyAdvantage and Currencycloud. Prior to that, she worked at JP Morgan Chase and General Electric. Arshi has an M.B.A. from Duke University and a computer engineering bachelor's from India's NITW (National Institute of Technology, Warangal).

Ritu Singh is an INSEAD MBA with global experience in leading sales, product, and marketing teams across industries. Solving for customer and organisation needs, using a blend of strategic vision, analytics, insight, technology, and commercial focus, to deliver value for clients and business.

As Regional Business Leader, Ritu is building the Emerging Markets Retail Trading business in StoneX, in markets across the globe. Ritu has built Global Agile teams and products, setting the product vision and roadmap and co-creating with cross-functional teams to deliver Client Experience, not just product features. Worked in Financial Services and Consumer Goods organisations. Ritu began her career as an FMCG Sales Intern, moving across roles with increasing responsibility and impact, in Commercial, Product and Brand Management, Strategic Marketing, Proposition Development, and Product Strategy. Having lived, studied, and worked in India, Singapore, France, and the UK, she has developed strong cultural sensitivity and enjoys working and learning with globally diverse teams.

Helen Smith has over 20 years' experience supporting transformation and growth in some of the largest tech-driven companies, before moving into FinTech 3 years ago. In late 2019, Helen joined Cashflows Europe Ltd. as the Chief Operating Officer where she is the architect and driver of the transformation and scaling strategy to grow revenue, reputation, and reach. She manages the day-to-day operation of the company with direct responsibility for key functions including Product, Proposition, Risk, Compliance, and Operations. In 2018, as Group Chief Operating Officer of AIM-listed cross-border payments company Earthport, she was responsible for driving the turnaround and growth of the company. A robust operating strategy alongside new enterprise controls and governance changes enabled disciplined scaling of business operations. A year later the company was successfully sold to Visa. Her early career took shape at EY where she travelled extensively supporting expansion and restructuring programmes and where she was quickly identified as having a talent for transformation. It was during this time that Helen says she truly got to understand the power and responsibility of leadership and that lasting, significant change is most effectively achieved through the authentic leadership of a capable and flexible organisation of diverse minds and backgrounds pulling in the same direction. Helen is fascinated and passionate about how technology continues to drive social and economic change for the better. Recognised for her energy, warmth and straight-talking approach, she is passionate about helping young professionals shape and progress their career potential. She played a key role in the launch of Sheryl Sandburg's 'Lean in London', is a coach to young talent in the creative industries, and a business mentor to young professionals in business and technology.

Akita Somani has over 20 years of international experience in retail financial services and payments, with companies such as Elavon (US Bank), Mastercard, Visa, Barclays, HSBC, and Citi, across roles in strategy, business development, and product development. Having lived and worked in five different countries, she brings a rich understanding of markets at different stages of development, and diverse cultures, across Asia, Europe, the Middle East, and Africa. She completed her Bachelor's from Delhi University and M.B.A. from XLRI—Xavier School of Management, both in India. Akita is passionate about people and relationships, and has the opportunity to drive an impact in this space as a Diversity, Equity, and Inclusion Champion at US Bank and being on the ASEAN Advisory Board for Women in Payments. She was also shortlisted as a finalist for the Women in Payments 2021 'Advocate for Women' Award for EMEA.

Andrea Sparke has worked in Fin Tech for over 18 years. She began her career with Morgan Stanley in London and pivoted into Technology in 2003. She has constantly been a top seller at every company she has worked for and been in the top 3 sales people globally. She now heads up Toppan Merrill's EMEA operation and is responsible for scaling their business and creating new business verticals. She has a very strong sense of justice and has always been a passionate advocate for women, equality, diversity, and inclusion as well as having a special interest in mental health and resilience and Psychological safety in the workplace. She is a mentor to two Fin Tech start-ups and is an environmentalist in her spare time.

Amrita Srivastava is the Head of FinTechs (W. Europe) at Mastercard, UK. Amrita Srivastava began her career in 2007 with a stint in banking giant Citi in New York, where she supported Mid-Corp Banking and then moved to Global Transactions Services. To broaden her career, she moved to Management Consulting with Kearney in London working on a variety of projects focused on digital and innovation strategy for challenger banks, retailers, and payment institutions. Recruited in 2018 by Mastercard to work on strategy and business development, Amrita led the FinTech strategy for Western Europe. Since 2020, Amrita is Mastercard's lead for strategic deals and investments with FinTechs across Western Europe. With a passion for supporting female entrepreneurs and businesswomen, Amrita was selected as one of 35 under 35 Women in business in the UK by Management Today and won the Rising Star of the Year by London Asian Business Awards in 2019. Amrita Srivastava has an M.B.A. from London Business School (UK) and studied Financial Economics & Math from Caldwell College (USA).

Ioanna Stanegloudi is a seasoned credit risk professional with 19 years in banking and management consulting. She possesses significant experience in corporate finance. Ioanna is the Co-Founder and Chief Risk Officer of Finclude, a pan-European scoring provider for individuals that assesses affordability and creditworthiness based on spending behaviour over transactional data. Ioanna has pitched Finclude throughout the globe gaining more than $800K in prize money, up to now. Finclude was one of the ten finalists of the Global Female Founders competition of Microsoft's Venture Fund, won the New Venture competition of NYU Stern, as well as the pitcHer competition of 2020's Grace Hopper Celebration. Finclude was in the Youth Solution Report for 2019 with the 50 solutions globally for the UN's SDGs. Ioanna was in the Greek "Fortune 40 under 40" (2019), is included in the NYC FinTech Women list (2020) and was recently honoured with the Greek International Women Award (2021).

Georgia Stewart is Chief Executive Officer of Tumelo. Georgia studied Natural Sciences at Cambridge; has experience from across the sustainable investment sector including equity investment analysis at Jupiter, clean tech venture capital at IP Group, and Business & Biodiversity projects at Fauna and Flora International (a conversation agency). She now runs a Bristol-based, financial technology scale-up, Tumelo. Tumelo's platform is designed to give investors and pension members visibility of the companies they are invested in and a voice on the environmental and social issues those companies are facing. Tumelo's software plugs into investment and pension to create more engaging and longer-lasting sustainable investment experiences for investors everywhere.

Dr. Erin B. Taylor is Founder of Finthropology, a research and consulting firm specialising in insights into human financial behaviour. She holds a Ph.D. in Anthropology from the University of Sydney, Australia, and has carried out ethnographic research in the Caribbean, Africa, and Europe. Erin's academic and industry research focuses on how innovation in financial services changes people's financial behaviour, and vice versa. She is the author of the book *Materializing Poverty: How the Poor Transform Their Lives* (2013, AltaMira). Erin has published chapters in books including *Money At the Margins* (2018, Berghahn Books), *Design Anthropology* (2017, Springer), and *Transformation Dynamics in FinTech* (2021, World Scientific Publishing). Along with Dr. Anette Br:løs she has been carrying out research on financial services aimed at women, publishing two reports in the Female Finance series (EWPN/Keen Innovation/Bank Cler). Erin and Anette are also co-leads of research at EWPN.

Sophie Theen is an award-winning Diversity and HR leader in FinTech and as the Chief People Officer in Oakam, her aim is to shift cultural paradigms within organisations and to champion diversity and equality using structured, disruptive thinking. Pre Oakam, she has led recruitment projects with Ford, General Motors, and IBM, before shifting to set up HR in early start-ups like Revolut and 11:FS. She is a recognised mentor, career coach for young women in tech, and a credited mental health coach. Active on the diversity agenda, Sophie also runs an HR community in Slack, Work Experience Programs for young women and as a People Advisor to new Founders of FinTech start-ups in London. She's been on the Women FinTech Powerlist in the UK for 3 years consecutively.

Jeni Trice is the Chief Executive Officer and Founder of Get with the Program, which partners with schools and businesses to deliver tech learning events that help encourage young children to get excited about coding and STEM. Jeni has over 20 years' experience working in technology and training as an SAP instructor and consultant, and now uses her alter-ego 'Professor' Trice to inspire children through engaging and inclusive in-person and virtual shows. Get with the Program uses a combination of storytelling, performance, and immersive learning to highlight the importance of STEM as a solution to real-world (and off-world!) problems for everyone. The programme aims to challenge stereotypes about who might be drawn to careers in tech in a format that is accessible to children from all backgrounds. All of their shows encourage inclusivity—from the choice of role models highlighted, right down to their female robot, Al (short for Algorithm)—and they also work hard to ensure their shows and activities work for SEN and neurodivergent students. Get with the Program provides a great opportunity for Corporate Social Responsibility initiatives, allowing businesses to link with schools to give back to their local communities and contribute meaningful support to developing the next generation of technology innovators.

Mel Tsiaprazis joined Bitstamp in 2021 and is responsible for commercial growth globally whilst working in tandem with partners to drive product and technology development. She has built her career on acquiring and employing new business models around the world, driving product and technology development as well as client growth. Prior to joining Bitstamp, Mel was Chief Operating Officer at Nivaura where she successfully drove the start-up to scale-up. As Chief Operating Officer at Crown Agents Bank, she led the bank's digital transformation and supported technology-focused business growth. She has also held senior positions at Mastercard, London Stock Exchange, and Lloyds Banking Group. A Harvard Alumni with a passion for doing good, Mel firmly believes that financial inclusion coupled with education can drive positive outcomes for future generations. She is also a champion for women in the workforce and an active supporter for inclusion and diversity—both in the workplace as well as local communities. She actions this belief through angel advice/investment in start-ups that support such vision.

Suresh Vaghjiani is Chief Executive Officer and Founder of Clowd 9, the world's first sustainable payments platform. Suresh has a long history of enabling innovation in payments including working with Monzo, Revolut, Curve, and Starling Bank from inception. Suresh has been an outspoken advocate for change in the banking sector and has been featured in numerous publications such as the Financial Times, Forbes, Raconteur, The Times, and many more. He and has represented the FinTech sector and the UK Government on a number of trade missions to Mexico, China including a historic delegation with the R. H. Lord Mayor of London to the southern hemisphere. Suresh brings a wealth of knowledge in global payments and has a substantial understanding of FinTech, throughout its complete value chain, with strategic knowledge on what works and does not work in various international markets in the highly regulated payment space.

Vanessa Vallely, OBE is one of the UK's most well-networked women and has provided keynotes on a variety of career-related topics for over 500 companies worldwide. Vanessa is also one of the UK's most prominent figures in gender equality and often provides guidance and consultancy to both government and corporate organisations who are seeking to attract, develop, and retain their female talent. Vanessa was awarded her OBE in June 2018 for her services to women and the economy.

At the height of her successful 25-year career in the financial services, Vanessa launched the award-winning WeAreTheCity.com in 2008 as a vehicle to help women progress in their careers. WeAreTheCity.com now has over 120,000 members and provides resources/conferences/awards/jobs to women across the UK. Vanessa is also the Founder of UK wide diversity forum Gender Networks. Gender Networks (formerly The Network of Networks) brings together diversity leaders from 85 cross-sector firms to share best practice on a quarterly basis. Vanessa is also the author of the book *Heels of Steel: Surviving and Thriving in the Corporate World* which tracks her career and shares 13 chapters of tips to succeed in the workplace.

Cindy van Niekerk is the Founder and Chief Executive Officer of Umazi, a corporate digital identity for corporation. As a South African born British national, Cindy has over 10 years of experience on the front lines of large-scale IT-regulatory projects with global financial institutions such as JP Morgan, HSBC, Barclays, Deutsche Bank, Lloyds, RBS, Scotiabank, Merrill Lynch, Northern Trust, NatWest and BNP Paribas. Cindy transitioned to the FinTech world in 2018, working with Marco Polo/TradeIX and Finteum. Cindy is an industry expert in blockchain technology and holds an Oxford Blockchain Strategy Certification by Said Business School as well as a Corda Developer Certification. As a compliance expert, she also holds an ICA KYC Compliance Certification.

Eleni Vlami has over 18 years working experience mainly in financial services and FinTech. She is currently Head of Account Management in Meniga. Her team is fostering relationships with Financial Institutions & Strategic Partnerships. The team is responsible for maintaining an ongoing collaboration with existing customers in more than 30 countries across the globe. Prior to that, Eleni was working in Citi & Piraeus Bank, supporting digital banking projects in Greece. Eleni was named in 'Women in FinTech PowerList' and shortlisted in 'Greek International Women Awards'. She is an active advocate on Diversity & Inclusion in FinTech industry, and she is also a Mentor in 'Women in Banking & Finance' (WIBF) and 'Reload Greece' organisations. She holds a B.Sc. Degree in Economics from National Kapodistrian University of Athens.

Dr. Ruth Wandhöfer has been instrumental in shaping the future of finance during her impressive career over the last 19 years. With a diverse career across regulatory policy development, banking, FinTech/RegTech mentoring, investing, and consulting she finds herself at the centre of the evolving digital ecosystem of players with the ability to advise, accelerate, promote, and enable technology players to become an integral part of the new financial ecosystem. Ruth was named as one of 2010s 'Rising Stars' by Financial News; named in Management Today's 2011 '35 Women under 35' list of women to watch and identified as one of the 100 Most Influential People in Finance 2012 by the Treasury Risk Magazine. She received the 'Women in Banking and Finance Award for Achievement' in 2015 and in 2016, 2017, 2018, and 2020 she was named on the global 'Women in FinTech Powerlist' of Innovate Finance (Senior Leader in 2020). She is a 2018, 2019, and 2020 Top 10 Global FinTech Influencer (FinTech Power 50). She balances this extraordinary career whilst raising her children and champions for a better work–life balance for parents and more support for women entrepreneurs.

Katharine Wooller has spent her career working in innovative start-up businesses, specialising in strategy and business development. Primarily focused on FinTech and banking, she has worked for technology-driven businesses in a number of sectors including investment banking, wealth management, hedge funds, and asset management. She has provided advisory services as a Non-Executive Director, focusing on disruptive FinTech and blockchain-related businesses. Dacxi has an easy and intuitive platform, and provides industry leading education to those wishing to get involved with crypto. Katharine joined the business in its early stages to launch in the UK and Europe. Dacxi has medium-term plans to offer other wealth opportunities via the platform, focusing on the technology sector. When not working hard on spreading Dacxi's message, Katharine can be found horse riding or long distance running.

Ben Wulwik is the Head of the award-winning Legal and Transaction Execution Team at OakNorth Bank. Ben joined the bank in March 2016 and since that time, the legal and Transaction Execution Team has facilitated several billion pounds of new closings to support UK businesses. In his time with OakNorth, Ben has overhauled the legal and execution infrastructure, investing in and developing OakNorth's automation of its lending products to facilitate a smoother execution process for customers. Ben leads a team of 18 across London and India and is proud of the role that the team play in the continued success of the bank.

Angela Yore is an entrepreneur, PR leader, and an influencer in the FinTech sector. Since co-founding SkyParlour in 2009, she has raised the profile of 100s of brands from dynamic start-ups to market leaders in the FinTech, tech, and ecommerce sectors. Listed on the Innovate Finance Stand out 35 Women in FinTech Powerlist 2020, Angela is a Chartered Institute of Marketing MCIM. Angela sits on various Advisory Boards including the Emerging Payments Association, FinTech Connect and the European Women Payments Network. She is the Chair of The Inclusion Foundation Executive Committee and a Governor of Wilmslow High School. Her latest project is being part of DIGISEQ's Non executive board. Angela is an international speaker and presenter with previous engagements at world-class events including Money2020, Finnovate, FinTech Connect, Internet Retailing, and Pay360. She believes passionately in citizenship, the power of communities and striving to make the world that little bit better.

Marta Zaccagnini is Program Manager for Europe at Village Capital, and she designs and implements investment readiness programmes that find, train, and support entrepreneurs solving problems in the region. Marta joined Village Capital after a decade working in humanitarian aid across Asia, the Middle East, Africa, and Europe. She is passionate about the potential for new businesses to cater to vulnerable populations and foster positive social change. Marta graduated with a B.A. in Anthropology and an M.A. in Human Rights from the University of Sussex and holds an M.Sc. in Urban Regeneration from the Bartlett School of Architecture, UCL.

Dora Ziambra joined the Azimo team in 2014 and brings a wealth of experience from across the financial sector. As Chief Operating Officer, Dora has been instrumental in building up Azimo's network of partners across more than 200 countries and scaling the business into new markets. It's a constantly evolving role as the company is growing so fast—day-to-day tasks can involve anything from banking relationships and strategic partnerships to fundraising and international expansion. She now also runs the Risk & Compliance and Operations teams across the group. Prior to Azimo, Dora has clocked up her fair share of air miles during her global career. She started out as a derivatives trader in Chicago, built her own options trading business in Germany, worked in international banking in London and Frankfurt, and joined a start-up advisory in Africa. Along the way, she has worked for the likes of ECB, Deutsche Börse, and PayPal. She holds a B.A. from Bryn Mawr College and an M.B.A. from INSEAD.

Contents

Contents

1

Purpose: Walk the Talk

Louise O'Shea, the Chief Executive Officer of Confused.com, a financial services comparison website, once said to me 'I love technology because it shows you the art of the possible'. She has inspired me to want to share why I think FinTech is in the perfect position to show the 'art of what is possible' for equality in workplaces in all sectors, and across the globe. Much to its detriment, there is and always has been a gross gender imbalance in financial services, in technology, and now in the FinTech space. This problem is now widely acknowledged, and it is becoming increasingly apparent that firms are being held back from being their best because of it. Furthermore, there is a growing awareness of the impact this imbalance has on the human experience of working in these firms. Where some businesses are still ignoring the issue of gender, diversity, and inclusion, dismissing it as a luxury item within their business strategy, many are realising just how pivotal these themes will be to their product creation, culture, success, sustainability, revenues, valuations, and ultimately profitability.

Over the years, I have led and participated in many discussions about gender balance and workplace diversity, and have seen positive actions that I want to share. I have interviewed over 150 women who work in the financial services technology field as part of my podcast series the 'FinTech with Nadia: The Diversity, Equity and Inclusion Discussions' of which the 'Women of Fintech' episodes are most established. I plan to present their advice as a blueprint for us all to follow should we wish to build inclusive teams.

N. Edwards-Dashti, *FinTech Women Walk the Talk*,
https://doi.org/10.1007/978-3-030-90574-3_1

I am a UK-based technology recruiter, turned Managing Director, turned Chief Customer Officer of the global recruitment agency, Harrington Starr. We specialise in placing technology and sales staff into the Financial Services space and I happen to be in one of the most successful Financial Services and more recently FinTech hubs in the entire world. This has meant that I have had the unique opportunity in meeting numerous senior partners in this space to learn about their culture, teams, missions, and goals of which addressing the gender imbalance has played a mounting part. Although I will draw from my global exposure, the key lessons I have learnt have been through my UK-based experience. I will be celebrating what I have seen globally, but my area of focus will be concentrated from the UK where I have been privileged enough to have shared so many conversations with the many, many women in this space. When I say women, I mean everyone who identifies as a woman.

Right now, in 2021, according to data produced by Price Water House Coopers, Computer Weekly Magazine, and WomeninTech.com, of all technologists that work in the UK only 17% of them are women. The worst part of this is that this dismal figure has remained stagnant for the past 5 years. Only 17% of FinTech leadership roles are held by women, and of the FinTech Top 50 only 5% of Founders are women. We have a big problem in technology and FinTech where businesses are not reflecting the gender balance of society. Why not? Why don't women want to join this groundbreaking industry? Why hasn't Financial Services, technology, and now FinTech ever been able to attract a more balanced representation of society? Why do women leave the industry after a few years? What is the lived experience for women? What can we do about it? How is it affecting the success of our businesses only having 50% of the world's perspectives, i.e. only men, at the table? What will this deficit mean for the future of the FinTech scene and its success? I will attempt to showcase how we can build a more gender-equal industry and why we haven't been able to so far.

In 2019 the advisory firm KPMG published data showing that female-led FinTech business saw 113% higher profits than those led by their male counterparts but still we face a huge disparity in representation. I don't need to focus on why it's so important to have a more balanced perspective in your workforce and why having a female perspective at your decision-making table is invaluable to your business. There is already so much data around the fiscal benefits of this let alone societal benefits. I will assume by picking up this book, that is your baseline and the 'how' we reach that goal is your next step. Jonas Karles, Chief Operating Officer and Co-Founder of Minna Technologies, a subscription management business committed to helping banks deliver a more powerful customer experience, said it clearly enough for all of us to relate to. When considering what we want for the businesses and teams we run Jonas allows us to think bigger. 'We set out in a mission to be the best and we strive for excellence in everything we do. I need to make sure that the workplace is a place of healthy debates and different backgrounds give different perspectives. We subscribe to having the best company culture, gender equality is part of it and brings forth different ideas. The workplace has more of a societal function than just performance and results, so we contribute to a better society as well'.

Over the decade of 2010s the topic of diversity has firmly found itself on the business agenda. It is certainly something that is spoken about but there simply isn't enough real action taking place. As an industry we have talked and talked and now I want to show how we all can 'walk the talk'.

This book will not be all be my words, instead I want to tell you about what the women of this community say about it's reality. I have spoken to the men of the industry too. It is my passionate belief that this imbalance isn't a woman's problem to solve but everyone's problem to solve and therefore we all need to work towards a solution together.

As the data from Price Waterhouse Coopers, Computer Weekly Magazine, and Womenintech.co.uk demonstrates there is a huge amount of work for the FinTech community to affect. There are many great steps forward that are being taken and if we can share these across industry and across sectors outside of FinTech, together we can be better and stronger through this learning. First, I will be explaining exactly what I mean by financial services and share my own experience of working with banks, hedge funds, asset managers, and the other traditional financial services environments that hire hired technologists. I will then discuss what the newer FinTech industry does and how its purpose is to harness technology, to automate and improve financial transactions. In turn I will cover what changes have been made possible. I will set out the problems women face in the workplace and explain the facts and figures to showcase the continuing issue of gender inequality within these industries.

We will need to include the yawning gender pay gap, current team compositions, the continuing board imbalances, and the dire statistics on funding barriers for women who try to start their own businesses in this space. I will share the words of people working within the financial services, technology and the FinTech space, from firms who are completely new start-ups and have just received their Series A funding, to those more established at B, those who are scaling up their companies at a pace and the financial services firms who have been here for years adapting to the needs of the marketplace. Every different perspective is relevant, and all together paints a true and fair picture of the discussion.

One of the most exciting points I will be making is the sheer potential the FinTech community has. How, if we all made the choice, FinTech could pave the way for a much more equal workforce. This is because as a community, FinTech is already steeped in change; it was built out of solving problems and proving itself successful in times of challenge. In particular, its growth out of the 2008 recession which has seen an enormous spike in new businesses and ventures solving many problems we didn't realise existed. The concept of building a more equal workforce isn't one that only considers gender, as it is important to note equality is about including everyone. One of the action-orientated leaders of the FinTech community is Regina Lau, who has worked in the payments space for over 20 years She is one of the women spearheading a movement I have supported many times, The European Women's Payment Network (EWPN). EWPN inspires, mentors, and empowers women in payments, through reports, networking events, webinars, and summits. Regina, one of the UK leaders of the group says, 'diversity isn't just about gender or ethnicity, it's about diverse perspectives and celebrating that'. These 'diverse perspectives' are central to the progress of the FinTech space.

It is important to note that those diverse perspectives come from everyone and from everywhere, including age, ethnicity, disability, culture, religion, sexuality, socio-economic backgrounds, gender orientation, and much more. I am an advocate of diversity, equity, and inclusion for all, however, for the purpose of what I knew I could tackle and where I could make an impact, I wanted to make change happen by tackling gender as a first step. Throughout this book I will use the terms diversity, equity, and inclusion and its key to note the comments of Lucy Heavens when thinking of the definitions. Lucy is the Marketing Director and a Board Member of Wealth Dynamix, a business that builds solutions for Wealth and Asset Managers and Private Banks. She is also the Co-Founder of a highly successful network called RegTech Women and with her 20 years plus experience within the industry she points out that 'too often diversity and inclusion are lumped together and it's important to recognise the difference between the two' if we give the concepts enough of a chance to really work. Lucy says that diversity is about 'recognising difference and acknowledging the benefit of having different perspectives involved in decision making' and that 'inclusion is where those differences are valued, and they are used to enable everyone to do better and thrive in their jobs'. Lucy reminded me of the popular phrase we hear in defining these notions where, 'diversity is when everyone is invited to the party, equity is where everyone contributes to the playlist and inclusion means everyone has the opportunity to dance!'

This book is my celebration of all the women in the FinTech community who wanted to spend time with me, participating in my podcast series about the unique challenges they face as women in business and in the world of financial services technology. Most importantly, this is about sharing their opinions on what still needs to be addressed to make FinTech environments a fairer, more equitable, and more inclusive place to work. I began inviting the women of FinTech onto my podcast series in 2019 to raise awareness of the challenges they face and to celebrate their wins. Every time I introduce my podcast I always say 'we are here today to walk the talk for change across the industry' because I wanted to ensure that we are sharing how action orientated we really are. I felt there were so many women who should have been given the opportunity to be more visible and given a platform to talk about their views, their feelings, their career journeys, and what they had personally done for the inclusion movement in FinTech. At the time there was no platform like this to share their advice across market at all and they had so much to say about what they had done to action change for equality. These women are senior leaders and C-level executives who have worked for years within the FinTech or financial services space. They shared their stories, their honest views, and have left such an impression on me and my podcast listeners, I felt the need to share their lived experiences more widely.

I wanted my podcast series to address the need for action and demand tangible results. This book is about that journey and how we have made steps forward for gender equality in the FinTech workplace and how others can use these lessons to make similar steps forward in their ecosystems.

These 150 women of my podcasts and the ever-growing community of FinTech women have become my network, my advocates, my teammates, and my mentors. We met for the purpose of the podcasts and all this happened to be during a time in my life where I, unknown to me at the time, desperately needed their support. As I went through a tough pregnancy and difficult birth of my first child during the COVID-19 pandemic, and then the pregnancy of my second child during the same pandemic I listened and learned from each podcast. What started as a typical podcast interview tuned into open, heartfelt conversations that I had never experienced within my male-dominated business or industry. The pandemic forced the industry to change, the word used widely was 'pivot' and the interesting realities of these pivots allowed for steps forward for workplace inclusion, as well as further anchors holding the gender debate back. I set out to share this all with you in the pages of this book. Not just through my eyes, but widely through the eyes of the great, the powerful, the wonderful women of FinTech. And a number of the men I would call 'allies'.

The world of work understands the importance of inclusion in the workplace and its widely known that diversity in your workforce is inextricably linked to profits; but so many are unsure of how to begin on their inclusion journey or what their first step should look like. Once I have explained my background, the world I work in and the people I call my community, I will be able to share exactly what has been done for gender equality in the workplace. I want to show what's stopped us taking it further and what must happen next.

Dr Jonathan Ashong-Lamptey is the host of the 'The Element of Inclusion' podcast; on his show he says everyone is on 'an inclusion journey', and that it doesn't matter where you are on that journey as long as you are moving forward, he adds everyone needs to travel at their own pace as long as there is a pace there should be no judgement. I first saw Dr Jonathan on the BBC news talking about tangible action for the Black Lives Matter movement and his mission to help a million people to make their workplace more inclusive. He has dedicated his career to making workplace authentic inclusion a reality through consulting, education, applied research and thought leadership.

The concept that workplace inclusion is a journey that you can travel at your own pace really captured me. In my job as a recruiter, I have spent nearly 17 years finding technologists jobs within the Financial Services sector and in this time, I learnt so much about where companies are on their own journeys. Some were not on a journey at all, but many were, and in the past ten years the conversations around inclusion have certainly gathered pace. I wish to shine a light on the tangibles that have taken place within the industry. In particular, companies and individuals that have escalated workplace inclusion and I plan to share the actionable 'take-aways' through lived experience and case studies. From this we can all learn and move along our inclusion journeys at a pace faster than ever before.

I started on my own inclusion journey a long time before I entered the world of work. I am lucky enough to come from a multi-religious, multi-ethnic, equalist, LGBTQ+ household. I was privileged enough to go to a mixed state London school where we all came from different backgrounds, cultures, races, religions, and economic circumstances and I rarely felt 'different'. On my first day at a London university in 2001 I was slapped with the realisation that being part of an ethnic minority, I would be discriminated against. This was through a nasty joke that I was too shocked and too slow to respond to. When I first joined the crowds of people that swarm up the escalators at Bank station at 7am every day in 2005, I was surprised by the absence of other women. Looking up and down the escalators I would count the women and it didn't take long. I had arrived in the City of London. I was going to be a recruiter and I was going to find technology people great jobs in the finance sector.

I didn't really appreciate what technology was back then. I had no idea that I was going to be part of one of the most exciting eras for technology in financial companies, and how they moved around or traded their money. Specifically witnessing the shift from the shouting and bartering day traders that you see in the films screaming Buy! Sell! to the automated trading systems that sat these traders at computers to move money quicker and more efficiently than ever before.

I barely knew what financial services were. It took me years to finally get my head around the fact that asset classes were simply different ways and speeds of moving money around with the aim of making more money out of it. Looking back, it's impressive how fast the industry changed and how dramatically the perception of the technology community within finance was raised. Back then, the technology teams within these financial companies were not seen as the core lifeline of the business, instead being considered 2nd class to the money-making front of house. Nowadays, technology is the money-making front of house, and no business will survive without it. I have loved playing my very small part in this revolution and now being part of taking technology in the financial space to a whole new inclusive level.

A keen graduate, I wanted to succeed and now in my much older years and understanding my personality type, I can say all I really wanted to do was to add value, gain approval, and feel like I had helped people. So, I put my mind to it, put in the hours, put in the effort, and learnt how to find people jobs in financial services technology. Those applicants happened to nearly always be men and those jobs nearly always had men as the hiring managers. This was the norm and when I did happen upon a female applicant, they rarely made it for an array of reasons that I now know to be unfair. As a compliant junior I did my time, I asked questions about what didn't sit right with me but kept quiet when the quick reason or rebuttal came to silence me and my concerns. I tried to live with that, and the only possible way I could live with it, coupled with the strain of the recruitment industry's own gender equality demons, was to completely block out any awareness of it from my mind as a coping mechanism.

2010 brought the opportunity for me to co-found the business, Harrington Starr. It was still recruitment and still technology and still in the financial service space, but this time with me as the right-hand woman to our Chief Executive Officer, Toby Babb. This meant that for the first time I was a person who could shape the business, how we interacted with each other as a team and how we interacted with the outside world. Then the real shift happened. I felt a responsibility to change what wasn't right and to talk freely about how to make that change happen and what the benefits would be.

Recruitment is a unique industry, often looked upon with scorn and historically filled with individuals who don't really take their job seriously and as such it has built itself a bad reputation. When we founded Harrington Starr we did so on the premise of honesty, trust, partnership, and community. We wanted not just to say we were different, we wanted to show people through our behaviours and actions how we were different. I wanted to build relationships with people when they were not currently looking for work or hiring a new member of staff so that when they were, they would already know, like, and trust me and be ready to partner long term. Building these relationships with a recruiter when people weren't looking for work or filling a job vacancy meant that I had to add value in other ways to build the engagement and therefore the community. As a business we started to hold events for potential clients to attend and these attracted hundreds of people across the FinTech community. We held them for free and our Chief Executive Officer invited speakers such as Khoi Tu, an ex-Google aficionado who wrote the book 'Superteams' and a Red Arrows pilot to speak about thinking clearly under pressure in business. For years I ran CV tailoring classes, careers coaching, recorded interview guide videos, and held events. One of these events was specifically for developers who attended to listen to four C-level powerhouses in FinTech to speak about how they began as developers and how they grew their career all the way up to C-level. The turnout for that was double the capacity of the one hundred seated room. We were truly adding value to people's careers, making them better versions of themselves, better managers, better leaders and we were building long-lasting relationships before we even spoke about our best skillset of recruiting.

This way of thinking meant that I could dream bigger, aim higher, and start to carve for myself a focus on authentic inclusion in our industry as a way of making it better. It became more than a focus; I now speak of it as a responsibility. As an experienced female within the recruitment industry who has spent 17 years working within the financial services technology space there is so much I have learnt and so much that I believe I have a duty of care to share. I soon realised that because of our level of quality, when speaking to applicants or clients looking to hire, I was learning about the industry I worked in. I knew products, I knew systems, I knew technologies, I knew about team composition, team compensation, board composition, and board compensation. I knew about plans to grow, the values, and cultural fits people were looking for. I was aware of who was getting promoted and who was getting overlooked and I could see who was leaving the industry and was in the best position to find out why.

I knew I had to draw conclusions from this and that I had to share this knowledge. I took a deep breath and stepped out of my comfort zone and began speaking at various events about what was happening for gender equality in the workplace and what the real barriers to making workplaces more equal were. I would build different workflows and operational plans to advise business leaders on how they could solve the gender imbalance problem in the industry. I certainly didn't need to explain why the gender imbalance hinders businesses; Chief Executive Officer's worldwide have acknowledged this for years.

It doesn't take much research to see the hundreds of articles and reports produced by consultancies and experts worldwide who state the facts and figures on the fiscal benefits. Laura Rofe, Strategic Partnerships Manager at PPRO Financial, a payments firm that helps merchants optimise the payment experience, puts it simply that 'shares rise with females on the board'. This business case for diversity and how it impacts profits and businesses' bottom lines is becoming clearer and clearer with Credit Suisse, Bloomberg, Allen, and Rosen producing evidence that we are missing opportunities worth billions of pounds by not tapping into this fact. It's now widely recognised that diverse workforces allow for better creativity, better innovation, and ultimately better commercial success and stability. Firms are more successful if they have gender parity within their teams and all this rhetoric is tied to the need to reflect their customer base and that customer base is the society we live in. This concept of differing views, different perspectives, different opinions, and ways of doing things brings a strength to the team and this strength of diversity is one of the many themes I set out to explore further.

Kimberley Lewis, previous Director, of Hermes Investment Management, a global leader in responsible investment agreed and said in her podcast back in early 2019 'companies are not likely to perform at their optimal ability if they do not have women in senior management' and yes there is so much to be read that backs up what she said in that podcast but who is recording the how? There is so much you can find on why but not much on the how. On a recent panel I was on with Sharon Doherty, the Chief of People and Places Officer at Finastra, a large FinTech offering a breadth of financial solutions. She said 'I'm bored! I'm bored we are still talking about this' making the progress we should be making. I couldn't agree more. We need to action the talk, or as I say, 'walk the talk'. Sharon is an advocate for change through actions and like many feels the fatigue of the 'all talk no action' problem we face.

My role as a recruiter, my visibility of the marketplace, and my podcasts have given me the opportunity to understand what is working and what isn't, what is expediting the positive change and what is hindering it. I want to discuss the 'how' to make our businesses, teams, workplaces more gender equal and share the learns I have gained from speaking to so many people through my role.

I want to unveil the truth behind what is actually happening in FinTech workplaces worldwide. I think that by being honest about where we are on our inclusion journey this will be able to help businesses outside of technology or finance too. I want to cement the new way of workplace thinking where businesses don't treat their inclusion wins as a trade secret but instead share and collaborate so we can improve as an industry. I believe this communal thinking will drive societal change and have a positive impact on the economy. I was introduced to this 'sharing learns across the industry' concept by Debbie Forster, MBE, of the Tech Talent Charter who has built her not-for-profit organisation on solving the inclusion problem in technology. Her not-for-profit organisation believes in the power of sharing the practical that makes sustainable change happen for inclusion in technology workplaces. She gathers data to ensure people are held accountable, that they focus on the whole ecosystem and can learn from one another to make the real change happen. In doing so she has brought together over 600 employers to work together to connect, convene, and amplify this message. Albeit not specialised to FinTech the Tech Talent Charter and the work Debbie does includes the FinTech community. When she says, 'everyone is in this together' and 'we accept there is no magic bullet', I've been spurned on to share what I know too. Her work is also all about the 'how'; the operational planning and education of the industry to make steps forward and she says those who sign up to her charter are 'people who get it and won't debate does diversity work but instead ask the question how do we make it work?'

I know this 'how' is so powerful and I believe the recruitment industry has a huge role to play to affect this. For me recruitment has always been a responsibility and never just about finding that one person one job. It was always about building long-term careers where people were delighted to accept positions and couldn't wait for their first day to really make an impact on that company. I've loved seeing how one engaged new employee can become the next future C-level member of staff defining strategy and plans for that business's future. If we multiply this and have lots of engaged people within the workforce, in turn we have stronger firms, in turn a stronger industry, in turn a stronger economy. The perception of recruiters and recruitment as an industry is far from this but my responsibility and my passion is this higher purpose to affect this 'bigger picture' of employee engagement, to make the FinTech industry better and stronger so that when I leave it, I leave a legacy.

There are many facets to employee engagement and Diversity and Inclusion is a central one. Companies, after realising that they hinder their own growth by not having a diverse workforce will introduce their sweeping statements of needing to hire more diverse candidates. Unfortunately, a big aspect of the problem is the ingenuine policies and unfounded proclamations of equality on social media. The authenticity of inclusion is key, and that authenticity is directly linked to any company's success, the industry's success, economic success on a societal scale, and ultimately a shift in age-old preconceptions. I knew early on that I had a huge part to play to ensure inclusive staff growth is done authentically, ethically, sustainably, and fairly. With this mission in mind the real learning of my career began.

I began speaking with the Chief Executive Officers, Heads of Business, Chief of Staff, Revenue Officers, and Chief of People about their firm's products or systems and who they were for, about their growth strategy and why this was intrinsic to their success, of course their plans for making this happen and more importantly where their challenges lay. People love to lay the blame or responsibility in the Human Resources department for any staff-related challenge such as growth, hiring, and especially the Diversity and Inclusion dilemma within the industry. Ultimately, I believe that if defining strategy sits with C-level staff, implementing that strategy is therefore shared across numerous departments, and that strategy simply cannot turn into a reality without the right team. Therefore, we are all part of the solution, we all need to be on an inclusion journey alongside Human Resources. We will explore how there are so many that fall at this first easy hurdle to leap over and why the choice to siphon off the responsibility to one department often leads to the failure of the inclusion mission.

There are so many examples of where companies and their leaders have the right intentions to affect their team composition but simply can't get to the results. So many have fantastic strategies to challenge parts of the inclusion debate but miss out on the basic foundations of other areas. As single entities I saw hundreds of firms across the industry trying to achieve workplace parity, I saw policies and actions that worked and goals that were left unreached. More importantly I saw that without doing this properly issues were often left unresolved that hindered the whole effort. I felt I needed to share what I had learnt and did so through my many talks at industry events, webinars, panel discussions, and roundtables each presenting workflows and step by step plans. In each of these, one clear theme rang true again and again was that of visibility. It was Regina Lau of the EWPN who said it best 'there are women and there's lots of them, it's about making them visible'. So simple yet so effective. People outside the industry had a perception of technology and a perception of financial services and those two put together amplified the perception that women don't exist here and even worse were not welcome. Having worked within this space and built wonderful relationships I knew I could make this visibility a reality for women everywhere not just on the scene. And so, I began my podcast journey.

I was self-taught and what I felt I could bring to my audience was authenticity. For my 'Women of FinTech' series I didn't want perfect podcasts, over scripted and cold. I wanted to celebrate the women of the FinTech industry, show that their career journeys were anything but straightforward and their achievements deserved celebration. I persuaded people to spend time with me by explaining that my mission was around relatable role models. I wanted to show people within the industry and those looking into the industry that these women were just like them as I felt that was more inspiring than those on pedestals that you couldn't feel a connection with. This connection made for heartfelt honest accounts of career growth within financial services, technology and more recently FinTech. As the podcast audiences grew and grew, I realised that there was so much more I could give back to the future generation of FinTech. So, I reached out to universities and put together talks for students at around 'demystifying FinTech' and showcasing what a wonderful career journey you could have no matter your background. From the University of Reading to the University of East London I loved these partnerships, and it wasn't long before I was talking to firms about setting up internships for the students who never would have thought the world of finance would have given them a chance. As my podcasts grew in popularity and momentum I began trying for a baby.

I had left this part of my life late, and I worried if perhaps I'd put my career first and left it too late. I spoke to many of my community about the 'having it all concept' and whether this was ever possible. When I knew I had conceived I was excited, then immediately I worried about what it would mean for me and my career. I realised that if I was worried when all I should have been was elated, then how many other women in the workplace were facing the same concerns? I decided to process my thoughts by educating myself on what men and women within FinTech had been exposed to during their family transition and so I began recording my podcast series 'the maternity and paternity stories of FinTech'.

Tribeni Chougule is the Head of Change Management, of Visa, the firm that powers a vast majority of our everyday financial transactions. She said eloquently in her podcast with me 'It's about storytelling and I believe exposure to other people's stories can help people gain self-awareness in terms of their own self-limiting and cultural barriers they might have themselves challenge and change their mindset'. It's exactly this challenge to my own mindset that I desperately needed. I wanted to see evidence that other people had prospered whilst starting their family and I wanted to know I could do both and do both well and without guilt—this is something I battle with to this day but at least I know I'm not alone.

It was incredibly liberating to speak to so many people across the industry who had already started their families and it hadn't ended their career, nor had they been demoted. It had absolutely changed them and learning about how to prepare myself for the birth of my daughter from a work perspective was invaluable for my confidence. My worries were not unfounded. FinTech, technology and finance each have had their own battles with retaining women in their workforces. What I learnt is that women wanting to become stay-at-home mums and choosing to leave the workforce at maternity age is not the biggest factor to the retention issues these industries face. It is, however, the perception. We know that the FinTech industry isn't alone in the world of work to lose a vast proportion of their women at maternity age, and we will explore this 'leaky pipeline' in depth when I discuss the reasons why we don't have a healthier gender balance in all our workplaces.

When the Coronavirus Pandemic hit the UK and threw us into National Lockdown in March 2020 I was 8 months pregnant and wanted to do everything possible to support the FinTech community in its survival. At the start of the pandemic there was so much unknown and the mere thought of everyone being asked to stay at home for our safety was such an alien concept. Stocks plummeted, share prices dropped, businesses failed, and firms that had been household names went bankrupt overnight. Everybody panicked, for their physical health, their monetary health, and then their mental health. In all this doom a sparkle of light was able to shine through. This is something I coined 'the humanity effect'. In the world of work, those who hadn't been furloughed or lost their jobs were able to pause and reflect. Feeling grateful for your job, your colleagues, and your family was all mixed up with the daily struggle of the huge challenges working from home, often with babies and children in tow. We started seeing the banks change their adverts on TV with slogans promising support and hope, we were given mortgage holidays and we saw millions released to support the hospitality sector worldwide. Julie Ashmore is the Chief Executive Officer of Rapid Cash a NatWest Markets funded FinTech that gives more freedom to invoice factoring. She described how 'COVID-19 meant that in a few days we needed 50,000 people working from home. We have learnt that this works, and it has allowed for a more diverse workforce' through a better technology infrastructure and way of reaching out to people wherever they were. We saw across the FinTech space a new way of looking at employees. No longer were staff replaceable, instead every person, their well-being and happiness was core to how each business would be able to stay afloat. Sonya Barlow, the Founder of a network for inclusion called Like Minded Females asked me to speak at one of her webinars early in the Pandemic about the need for us all together to survive, drive forward and later thrive. FinTech was born out of resilience, and I believed that we would find ways to overcome the enormity of the challenge. As such, to support the community I decided to start a podcast series called 'the Talent Surgery'. I set about speaking to people across the FinTech space about their people strategy, how they were supporting their staff and what their strategies were to 'pivot' their business to ensure its survival. The fact of the matter was that a seal had been broken for flexible working and working from home. In previous years managers, leaders and Chief Executive Officers of businesses would have felt that productivity would be shot or that they simply couldn't trust their staff to have such flexibility, now there was no choice and we still worked, and we still pushed businesses forward.

I am only scratching at the surface when I mention these huge societal and working norm shifts but they are incredibly relevant to how we can all 'walk the talk' for gender equality in the workplace. One thing that became so evident to me over these initial podcast years of mine was that storytelling of people within the FinTech space was teaching me about how much this industry is capable of in terms of driving change. When looking at how women were represented in the wider sense, the UK government made a catalogue of errors throughout the Pandemic, from abandoning the annual gender pay gap report in April 2020 to producing a 'Stay at Home' poster in January 2021 depicting women as only homemakers, home schoolers and cleaners with zero acknowledgement of what else women represent. The poster was quickly withdrawn and labelled as a mistake, but the damage has been done time and time again. It is so clear to me that if we want to address workplace equality, we need to do it ourselves. Companies must drive this, and I believe some are starting to and some more want to and want to know how to.

The minute leaders understand that diversity is linked to profits, the conversation moves to the 'how do we get there?' and that's incredibly exciting to me as I know that this book will help share so much of that which will drive real, actionable, results, and change.

To really embed this change we must be honest about where we are right now, how far we have come and what's stopping us from going further. I want to unveil the truth about what really holds back gender equality in the workplace and pose solutions to how we can step forward. There is so much to consider from what does equality looks like in the workplace? What does it look like at board level? What about equal pay? At whose door does the responsibility lie to achieve it? Who will be responsible for keeping it up? The answers are all within what is happening right now in FinTech; the successes, the fast starts, those that trail off, those that stagnate, and those who are truly building sustainable and inclusive workforces. My podcast series has given me the unique position to be able to report on these key facts, through storytelling, evidence building, and case studies. Moreover, I pledge to be authentic to the cause and showcase where companies have gone wrong. Where I will show that many firms want to move towards better workplace equality and an evolution is taking place, I also need to be clear that unfortunately many businesses don't tackle the reality of what's needed but instead try and tick boxes or implement strategies that simply won't work to appear they are doing what they should. Once again, I will say, gender is only one aspect of the entire diversity, equity, and inclusion spectrum and along my journey I started my 'Humans of FinTech' series to begin my education and storytelling of these wider facets.

Many businesses have hardworking marketing departments that help portray them as inclusive environments without having genuine policies or practices to back this up. The problem of appearing inclusive when in reality a company is not, is a genuine issue we face. This is no surprise because what we are talking about it is a complex mission where we must challenge expectations, norms, status quo, and societal perceptions. By not reaching authentic equality in our workplaces, we affect and hold back us all, therefore all of us need to be involved to reach our mission. I must be absolutely clear this is not a woman's problem it's a human problem and for all our sakes we need to rectify it. I don't claim to be an anthropologist, philosopher, or sociologist instead I want to report my findings having worked in this space for 17 years and worked purely with people and how they build their teams, retain their staff, invest in their people, and promote their star players. We all need to be clear that when Lax Narayan, a prominent technologist at Toronto Dominion Securities, a Canadian Bank and financial services provider, said, 'through my ten years in financial services I never felt held back by being a woman but I can't help but notice I'm always the one or two in the floor or department and I wanted to help to change this and attract more women to our company'. She was talking about what we all need to do to make our business more attractive to women. She spoke about parenting support, flexible working, and psychological safety at work. These are all things we will explore amongst many other points further in the pursuit of really being able to bring your 'whole self to work' no matter who you are and where you come from, to be like Lax and 'feel very appreciated'.

My long-term aim is for this to not be a conversation but an expectation, this cannot be a luxury item but instead a necessity to a successful business. The belief is for equality in the workplace, where men, women, and people of all genders, cultures, ages, religious, sexual, socio-economic backgrounds are promoted equally, paid equally, and given the chance to add their own unique value to the business; but we are not there yet. I want to showcase the winners, the success stories, and most importantly the reality of what is needed to truly achieve what many companies are setting out to do.

In doing so I will debunk the generalisations, assumptions, and several things we simply take for granted or accept because we always have in the workplace. This should be a journal of how companies can truly build great teams, sustainable teams, and happy profitable environments. For me the best way to articulate what I would love to achieve was said by Dr Louise Ryan, the Head of Portfolio Management at Close Brothers, a merchant bank providing lending, deposits, wealth management, and securities. In the final thoughts of her podcast, she said 'I challenge the audience - are you providing support to your cohort? Can you see a gender balance? Could you be doing more to help a colleague out or someone in your network?' If we could all challenge ourselves to turn these pages into further action, then real change will happen and this topic won't be boring and over discussed but one of celebration and action where in years to come we can look back with pride and then look forward to our children, in the hope that their workplaces are better off, their careers are better off, and they are better off because of it. Together let's 'walk the talk'.

2

Mission: What Is FinTech?

I describe FinTech in a unique way. I am extremely optimistic about the potential opportunities this newish industry has and will continue to have. I look at the industry emotively and with excitement because I believe it can change workplace gender equality for the good, for all of us. It is not just about the world in which we work, it is about that impact on the world in which we live and the potential impact this industry has on both. I want to be clear about the terms I use and what you visualise when I say FinTech or traditional financial services or financial services technology.

Traditional financial services are typically the institutions that have been around for years, often steeped in history and named after someone's great great grandfather. Banks, asset managers, hedge funds, worldwide stock exchanges; the big names you see on those tall buildings in Canary Wharf. They have spent hundreds of years in some cases saving money, moving money, and further investing money, largely for the wealthy or on behalf of big corporations. These institutions are large, established, well-known names that are highly regulated. Since the subprime mortgage crash of 2007 and the following 2008 recession the regulations had to go through the roof to prevent any such over lending from happening again.

The role of technology within the financial world has grown from the first steps of digitalising cash in the 1950s with the introduction of the credit card, to the 1980s mammoth mainframe computers which were used to record financial transactions worldwide. Over the past 50 years, technology has played an ever-growing role within this space. It has been fuelled by the

© The Author(s), under exclusive license to Springer Nature
Switzerland AG 2022
N. Edwards-Dashti, *FinTech Women Walk the Talk*,
https://doi.org/10.1007/978-3-030-90574-3_2

evolution of how we handle money and innovations around the solution providing. I loved partnering with various financial institutions, namely the exchanges and or trading institutions in the 2000s and beyond, to help them grow teams upon teams of technologists to build their new electronic trading systems that were taking over the long-established voice trading as a means of monetary transactions. This rate of technology change has gotten faster and faster with every technology improvement, every challenge this sector has faced and every time anyone has been able to think of a more efficient way of doing it. It is clear to see the rate of change is rapid and the potential is never ending.

The first use of the word FinTechcan be dated all the way back to the 1980s to describe any financial services technology. More recently we tend to use it to describe all businesses that have automated what the traditional financial services have done within their core business. These businesses took the opportunity of the 2008 recession, this period exposed the many failures of the traditional financial services processes and built their organisations to do the job better, faster, cheaper, and in many cases to make the industry more accessible to all. In the majority they have set out to take one or two elements of the traditional banking processes and set out to improve it by building a more elegant solution to reach more people than ever before. Hannah Lana Preston who began her career in lending, underwriting, and development finance is now a Commercial Strategy Advisor for the successful FinTech, Minna Technologies. She says 'FinTechs make financial well-being accessible to all people and that really inspires me about FinTech, I love the fact we are empowering all consumers not just the wealthy ones'. Minna is an example of a FinTech that is delivering a subscription management service that drives a more widespread adoption of technology making banking safer, simpler, and more valuable in people's everyday life.

Everyone will recognise the new Digital Banks and payment methods that have appeared since 2010 from Monzo to Starling bank, Metro Bank to Klarna. Through reading this book there will be names of organisations that you will no doubt recognise and others that are at the embryonic stage of their journey. As in other industries there are several nuances used to describe whereabouts on the journey the particular company is. The organisations at their inception looking to build are known as the start-ups and these are normally seeking funding or have just received their first financial injection to get off the ground. They will have a product with a mission, a purpose and a plan and will have had the Founders and C-level staff go to Venture Capitalists and Investors to pitch their ideas for money to help them set up the foundations of their business by receiving monetary investment called series A funding. The FinTechs that get off the ground and experience early success can grow at an alarming rate to meet the demands of their new customers, and are known as the 'scale-ups'. Often these firms will apply for more funding to afford themselves this growth known as series B. Even in early 2021 right in the middle of the pandemic we have seen so many success stories where UK FinTech's have received millions of pounds in investments to grow to their next stage. Often the fiscal goal of these FinTechs is to reach unicorn status where they remain privately owned and have a valuation exceeding $1 billion.

FinTechs have successfully made banking mobile, they have improved the security of our financial data and they are putting the consumer first in their propositions. To put the potential of this industry into context, in 2013 just over $4 billion was invested into FinTechs. Only a year later this had tripled to $12 billion and in 2019, $137 billion was being invested. Pre-pandemic, all reports suggested that the FinTech market would grow by an astonishing 25% year on year and by 2022 would be worth $309 billion. The pandemic has lead to a hiatus but I will be showing in the next few chapters that as I write, FinTechs and their work with financial institutions is proving resilient in the face of the pandemic.

Dora Ziambra, the Chief Operating Officer of Azimo, a FinTech promising a faster, cheaper, and more accessible way of transferring money abroad, talks about how challenge leads to innovation and even the pandemic has paved the way, giving FinTechs the opportunity to disrupt further due to circumstance. She spoke to me at the start of the pandemic in early 2020 about how FinTechs may offer a better way of doing business, but they still need to gain trust. She spoke about how 'FinTechs have a general challenge with trust. Most of us are digital natives, most people trust the big banks, the ones where you can see the big buildings in Canary Wharf' and customers are sceptical before they start using a digital service. She went on to say that she felt that this attitude was changing over time and that people are more and more inclined to use digital services for money and the crisis was allowing her to 'see an acceleration because now people don't have many other options, so they give it a try'. Simply because of the ease, security, and accessibility of her product.

It has been fascinating to see the financial services sector shift in focus; from being almost an exclusive secret society that enjoyed the mystique of complexity, to an industry that now prides itself on simplifying its processes for all to understand and be a part of. Just like the Azimo story, the concept of disruption is an empowering one and now that these many FinTechs seek to enable and partner with traditional financial services to improve their ways of working makes the potential so much more. The challenge the pandemic posed has allowed for firms such as Azimo to thrive through their mission of getting money to people missed by the traditional financial institutions known as the 'underserved'.

Mel Tsiaprazis, the Chief Commercial Officer of BitStamp, is another person on a mission to change the financial world and who has access to it. BitStamp is the original Cryptocurrency global exchange who pride themselves on their ability to provide reliable trading of cryptocurrencies. Mel's personal driver is that 'money is about humanity and the wealth of ideas not the wealth of funds', meaning that her entire career journey has been dedicated to leaving a positive imprint and a legacy. When talking about the traditional ways of dealing with money she admitted that they have been 'really over complicated, really inefficient and dare I say it old fashioned, often run manually by humans who lead highly digitalised lives. We work with people rather than disrupt them'. Mel's collaborative nature and purpose within the business is paving the way for their successes.

I remember the early 2000s where the technology and business were two separate entities in financial institutions. They were two entities that didn't communicate well and were not culturally aligned. This seems such an alien concept now as in our world, how on earth can any business function without technology at its core? As a society we have come so far to accept that technology plays a key role in all aspects of our lives in ways that are easy to use, saves us time, and are cost efficient, ranging from our home security to how we listen to the radio to bringing our families together even when we are based all over the world. It is no different in the world of finance. These FinTechs that have grown to challenge banking and traditional financial services' modus operandi and have ended up building out their own ecosystems within their firms. In turn, enabling those traditional institutions to do more. Historically there was a hierarchy in the traditional institutions where the business brought in the money and the technology teams simply supported them, now without technology there is no money. As part of this shift, we have seen technologists rise in prominence and become Chief Executive Officers of their own companies focused on being lean and efficient.

These new disruptive FinTech ecosystems have paved the way for a lot of people with different skill sets to be part of this new world. Trading is now run by developers and mathematicians creating algorithms and trading strategies and they are supported by a wealth of knowledge and communication that has numerous responsibilities and job titles. These FinTech ecosystems are made up of the typical technology roles of developers, analysts and support technicians, but they are not alone. To add to this we see legal, compliance, security, marketing, product, finance, and a number of other important roles across these businesses. The plethora of skills at work in the technology departments are no longer only the perceived coding positions or number crunching. The world of FinTech is about opinions, perceptions, communication, and most importantly diversity of thought. We see new titles of Chief People Officers where we did not see them before, digitally run marketing departments, pure finance roles being about presenting new ideas to the board and those being taken on as new product streams. And it is changing so quickly.

As a recruiter in the space, I've learnt so much about the value of communication and how everybody, technical or not, contributes to a FinTech. The real power is in explaining the technical complexities in a way everyone can understand. The need for all these different skill sets has allowed for the industry to have the potential to be inclusive in a way we haven't previously seen or ever expected, and this is why I'm so excited to work within the space and why I believe my role as a recruiter holds huge responsibility to help foster this change. As Lax Naryan of Toronto Dominion Securities said, 'You can do many different roles across the financial services and FinTech community now' and 'we are all working on making it more accessible' to be able to attract people with different opinions to make the industry stronger.

FinTechs are all about products and products need to serve customers. Zoe Newman, the US Managing Director at Capital on Tap, the business dedicated to supporting small businesses through their business credit cards, is a huge advocate for variety. She didn't have a Computer Science degree and she charts her success as a long-standing member of the Capital On Tap team because of her belief that 'you can take a lot of skills you learn in any course and utilise those in a career in FinTech'. As a geography graduate, she speaks highly of her analytical and problem solving skills. She celebrated her teammates highlighting that most of them came from generalist backgrounds and were therefore able to bring a 'dynamic range of skills' which allowed for a fresh perspective. This way of thinking and team building has meant that as a business they can totally focus on 'what the customers want rather than this is how a bank does it'.

This desire to understand what the customer needs is a huge FinTech theme that again has driven the need for different perspectives within any successful firm's ecosystem. This diversity of thought allows them to service their expanding customer base better. I spoke with Rahma Javed, a woman who has dedicated a large part of her career to the financial services space and now works as Director of Engineering of Deliveroo, the fast food delivery firm on their own mission to revolutionise how we order fast food. When we spoke about this concept of technology becoming more accessible and including more people she said 'We are all trying to achieve diversity of thought, diversity of perspective and diversity of opinions because we feel collectively we will come to a better decision because we can look at data from various angles'.

We have to be clear on how far we have come. Traditional financial services did not think this way. This desire to reach out to previously untapped markets has paved the way for untapped thinking. I have seen how this has opened the door for diversity of thought which naturally is about diversity of people within business and herein lies the strength of gender diversity within business and all diversity and inclusion. In an industry that Alice Leguay of Clim8 Invest so aptly describes as 'delivering delight to customers', we need to acknowledge that delight takes research, takes experience and takes people-focused problem solving. Alice is the Chief Commercial Officer of Clim8, a sustainable investment platform that helps consumers invest exclusively in solutions to the climate crisis. In 2020, they received over £4.4 million worth of funding and has proved to be incredibly successful by reaching out to people by simply saying, you can 'fight climate change with your savings'. Just one example of how FinTechs are tapping into emotion and humanity.

Most people will identify FinTech with those who automate a long drawn out banking process, I aim to show that many challenge the status quo in a wider sense and once you start to question what you have always accepted, the potential is endless.

The changes we are seeing for the billions of people worldwide who were previously called the 'unbanked' or 'underbanked' have been huge. These people don't use traditional banks, they are often paid in cash and definitely won't have a credit history. This reduces their options in today's world where the digitalisation of cash is paramount. This is not just about savings, mortgages, or getting a mobile phone contract, it's about independence, equality, and giving people rights in their everyday lives. These people, from a business point of view, are potential customers and different ways of reaching them have grown with the FinTech community. A great example of this comes from Erica Gibson, The Global Head of User Research at SumUp, when she said 'we believe in the everyday hero and we learn from them so we can serve them better!' SumUp is a perfect illustration of the sheer potential FinTechs have to change the world we live in for the better. They set out to empower business owners who previously only accepted cash. Their solutions enable these business owners to accept card payments whether in-store, in-app, or online in a simple and cost effective way. Life changing for the millions of small merchants worldwide.

Looking at people who join these FinTech companies, career pathways have never been so interchanging than the opportunities we have seen recently. FinTechs aren't governed by red tape and corporate traditions of 100 years. Therefore, you don't need to be from a Russell group university, have won a boat race or be over 40 before you make partner. A great example of how quickly FinTechs are changing the status quo is the well-known builder of next-generation financial solutions, 11:FS. Within 4 years of 11:FS's founding they had over 150 staff making waves in their specialism; creating digital transformation for banks. Their Founder and Chief Executive Officer, David Brear, said we are trying to 'usher in digital in financial services and have a lot of fun while we are doing it'. I met David when I invited him into the Harrington Starr offices in late 2019 to record a Maternity and Paternity Stories of FinTech podcast. When explaining his version of hyper scaling his business that would change the way we bank, he focused largely on people and culture. I loved hearing about building a business where everyone is tied into the mission, the values, the purpose. Naturally David spoke about how much time he invested into culture and people being in line with the '11 out of 10' concept the business was founded on.

Looking back to the earlier 2000s when I started working with technologists in this field, did we ever discuss the mission of a Bank when they were considering working for them or the purpose of a vendor building financial products for the banks? Probably not. Not because I was junior and not doing my job properly, it was because back then missions or purpose in business were not held in the regard they are within this industry today. The interview process for a new hire was focused on can you do the job, not do you want to, and how passionate will you be within this team and what new ideas can you bring. Instead, it was largely fit in and complete the task assigned to you. Therefore, the job was the job, it wasn't necessarily putting you first and on a career path to change your life. I searched high and low for the career-building roles I could place technologists in. I loved changing the lives of people by helping them secure a long-term career opportunity that I knew would give them their own mission and purpose.

The arrival of FinTech allowed for all of this to change across the entire industry and to the benefit of everyone applying to be part of it. We now talk about people falling in love with their jobs because it's their passion, they are aware of what the business is trying to do in the grand scheme of the marketplace, and they want to join their mission and make a difference. This is now apparent in the traditional institutions too.

Mission-led FinTech's are incredibly exciting to work with. The people looking to join them can do so from all sorts of backgrounds because to disrupt you need to keep innovating. To keep innovating you need new ideas and if we keep building teams with the same people and personalities we will simply come up with the same ideas. This revelation in the FinTech world has allowed for the diversity of thought concept. Julie Ashmore of NatWest's FinTech, Rapid Cash, explored the reality that for this diversity of thought to work you need to 'create the social environment' that allows people to truly 'bring their whole selves to work'. She discussed in her podcast that diversity of thought only works if you are not feeling the pressure to be like everyone else and we all have a responsibility to make our environments safe for this. The constant need for innovation within today's financial world drives this potential for true diversity of thought. The reality is that FinTech businesses are now seeking out a new mix of personality type in their teams, people of different backgrounds, cultures, religions, gender, and I could go on and on. The theory makes sense of course, but the reality is far more complex and I plan to explore this further through my own mission of gender equality within the workplace and the barriers we face to achieve it.

Nim Haas, an award-winning marketing specialist and 25-year veteran within the financial services and more specifically payments space, brought the Banking and FinTech worlds together when she told me about how the 'banks are focusing on trying to catch up in their digital transformation, but this culture of innovation will be a hard one for them'. Nim has worked for some of the major influencers of today's FinTech Community and having set up her own Marketing consultancy, TechFuse, is able to help businesses position themselves appropriately within the space. Her knowledge has meant she has won multiple awards in the space and was even recognised by Innovate Finance, an independent. not-for-profit FinTech community, in their yearly Women of FinTech Powerlist naming her as one of the Standout 35 in 2019. She sees the power of change being in authentic propositions, authentic culture creation, and authentic inclusion. Where businesses are global already or growing globally the need for these different perspectives within a safe environment becomes more important than ever.

For many, FinTechs are simply automating traditional financial services' processes and making money out of it. For me, I have tried to encapsulate the humanity, the inclusion, the innovation, and the diversity opportunity FinTechs have opened up. It is about all people and affecting so many more people than have previously been reached. There is so much potential here, but the reality is that we haven't embraced it fully yet. This potential is something I want to showcase further in my next chapter so we can all see the opportunity in how these businesses are working and how they are affecting the wider industry.

3

Mindset: Innovation and Transformation

The FinTech culture of innovation is closely aligned to what I call the 'FinTech Mindset'. There is a wealth of evidence demonstrating how the FinTech community is using this culture of innovation to build resilience within their teams and in turn allow for faster adaptations, more efficient delivery and products that delight their growing customer base. It takes a certain individual and certain mindset to be truly successful within it because they need to be prepared for high rates of change and furthermore demand it. As previously discussed, we know that modern FinTech is all about ensuring that traditional financial processes and methodologies are made more efficient, simpler for the consumer and are driven by a purpose. For this to happen every team within a business is dedicated to their mission and need to be constantly looking for improvements in their methods. Lots of firms look at completely overhauling the traditional systems altogether and are creating new ways of processing payments, lending money, or investing. Just taking into consideration the new international credit cards, the peer-to-peer lending or crowdfunding we see advertised and read about on a daily basis shows us how far we have come.

To be part of this ever-changing world, there needs a mindset where challenge is positive, debate is key and most importantly questioning is fundamental. I wish to explore why this sector is ripe for the change we seek to drive for workplace inclusion.

As someone who finds technologists' jobs across the FinTech and financial services technology space, it is very clear to me that job descriptions have

© The Author(s), under exclusive license to Springer Nature
Switzerland AG 2022
N. Edwards-Dashti, *FinTech Women Walk the Talk*,
https://doi.org/10.1007/978-3-030-90574-3_3

never ever meant so little and softer skills such as communication, creation, and resilience are far more important to someone's potential success within a business. This is not to say experience and skill sets are not valuable, but less so than we have seen historically. Being able to handle unexpected situations is an example of this and when Chief Operational Officer, Adrienne Muir, joined Voxsmart she valued the chance to build something. VoxSmart is a RegTech that turns a company's communication data into useful information about employee activity. On Adrienne's first day she walked into a room with an empty desk and was told she may have to wipe it down. She was then taken to a nearby computer shop and asked to pick out what computer she wanted. She says of the experience, 'I know some people would love that and others would just freak out'. Adrienne loved it because she knew she was walking into a business that she could bring her own unique perspective. 'I was getting to build something from scratch, and I knew how I wanted to treat people in an organisation'. She relished the opportunity to bring something new and, in her podcast, specifically spoke about bringing in people to the business based on their potential, their values and the way in which they think. She works incredibly hard to build a safe environment where people feel they can bring their viewpoint to the table and believes that to drive a business to success you need people to ask questions and difficult questions at that! What Adrienne saw on her first day is increasingly becoming the norm for new starters embarking on new opportunities.

FinTech businesses have been popping up world-wide with an impressive pace since 2010. Each of them with their own unique mission and purpose, have had people at the helm who want to make change happen and who want to do things differently. Having spoken to so many Chief Executive Officers of these businesses, I know that a lot of this drive has come from their 'lived experience'. They have faced a problem and their decision to solve that problem was not just to solve it for themselves, but for many others after them. It was exactly this concept that drove Ioanna Stanegloudi, the Chief Risk Officer and Co-Founder of Finclude, a company dedicated to offering EU citizens fair access to credit. Ioanna, the recent winner of the Greek International Women's Award in Business and Entrepreneurship 2021, was driven by the challenge she personally faced by losing her financial history every time she moved across borders. She was made acutely aware that the traditional credit assessment system was archaic and has now built a business to offer other ways to assess credit. These ways are more inclusive and extend beyond the initial problem that she was solving. Explaining that credit is based on your financial history she said, 'we give a chance to people who don't have credit, financial inclusion is more than relocating financial immigrants'.

By using transactional data 'we help first time home buyers with no credit files, or a student just out of university who got her first job'. The business was born out of a problem and this founder decided to provide an alternative solution to this problem.

Within a lot of these FinTechs we have seen traditional processes of finance being shortened and the phrase 'removing the middleman' has been used widely to highlight how less cumbersome these new solutions are. Again, to be the creator of something new, or the team that constantly seeks opportunities for further efficiencies this takes a certain mindset. One that relishes in this challenge, who questions the norm again and again, who enjoys healthy debate and as I like to say, seeks out the problems as every problem with the right mindset is an opportunity in disguise. When I speak to university students about the wonderful career opportunities that lie ahead of them in the world of FinTech, I always focus on this point and ask everyone to reframe their thinking so that they can thrive in this environment.

Taking this a step further, Dr Ruth Wandhöfer, partner at the FinTech focused Venture Capital firm Gauss Ventures, says that 'there are lots of people coming out of the banks and they are in the sweet spot, they know the industry well, they understand the technology and have a passion for this as well as see the opportunity for new business models'. Ruth's expertise within the space spans over 20 years and she sits on multiple boards within the Financial Services and Technology industries. With her knowledge she speaks about the rate of change possible in FinTechs compared to that of the traditional Financial Services world and how exciting it is for FinTechs and their founders to drive automation, agility, and showcase 'how can you be lean in terms of a cost exercise'.

This mindset of challenge and change has allowed for new roles being created across the industry. Roles we have never heard of before and roles solving problems we had not previously identified. It's incredibly exciting to see the new skill sets required for these new roles, as many of them technical as they may be, require much more interpersonal skills than we have previously seen. A great example of this comes from Kimberley Lewis, a Director at Hermes Investment Management, when she said, 'I never expected to work in an investment firm having the views I have, the role I have didn't exist 15 years ago, ultimately it's the analysis of social good'. Kimberley's background is diverse having worked in politics as a campaign worker to an attorney of Capitol Hill and now within Financial Services. She prides herself on her ability to bring these experiences to her job. Her role is focused on environmental, social, and governance issues with a view to improve long-term corporate value for clients' holdings. There are many other roles being created and areas within FinTech that are growing at a speed never seen before. Innovation, Cyber Security, Data, DevOps, and Product just to name a few areas. In addition to technology and corporate social responsibility growth, we also see international growth paving the way for different skill sets and experiences. As Zoe Newman, the US Managing Director at Capital on Tap points out, 'when you are defining your international strategies you want people with various cultural backgrounds'. And herein lies the real opportunity and why I believe FinTech can become a beacon of change for the gender equality debate in the workplace.

Many FinTechs start as an idea, often solving a problem. As their mission and purpose gains momentum, they grow in size in response to a growing demand of consumers. As that consumer base expands so does the need for their team to service all those different consumers. What I am describing harks back to what Julie Ashmore, the Chief Executive Officer of Rapid Cash, said when she stated that 'for a business to be successful it needs to reflect the markets they are serving'. Diversity can therefore be looked at far more broadly within FinTech. She goes on to highlight that 'when you bring lots of diverse people with different backgrounds, experiences and belief sets, that's where I feel we build the strongest teams. There is very clear evidence that the most diverse teams are the most successful'. As the demand for wider perspectives elevates, we are able to use more varied experience levels, backgrounds, academics, personalities, character sets, and skill sets as a starting point for when we are looking to hire people into the industry. Again, there is a huge opportunity here for us to take this much further, to affect not just the gender imbalance in the industry but make broader the neural and cultural diversity we currently see in teams.

Hiring people from different backgrounds and skill sets has needed something to tie them together, a mission and a purpose to act as a root for 'culture creation'. Kate Bohn is an Innovation Evangelist with experience of working at Lloyds Banking Group, Deutsche Bank, and Citi Bank. She won 'Woman in Technology' in the Leadership category at the 'Banking in Technology' awards run by FinTech Futures in 2020. She has a wealth of knowledge in the space and loves how the FinTech mission is 'bringing people around [a] collective purpose and when supporting that talent, you can become part of the magic that results off the back of that'. She believes that if you have a 'collective purpose' that people are bought into, whatever their background, then 'there are boundless opportunities for discussion and creation'. These opportunities have become the basis of many new mission-led FinTech businesses.

As a reminder, these missions are incredibly meaningful and important. We are seeing careers that are forever changing, technology that is forever improving, changes to the way we save money, spend money, transfer money, and so much more. Talking of the financial services industry, Louise O'Shea, the Chief Executive Officer of Confused.com, said 'there are so many opportunities to do it better and make a significant difference to an individual's life by saving them money and by improving their choices. For me you've got to have a good reason to get up in the morning, you've got to have a good reason to leave your kids and go to work and that's a very good reason'. We must remember the sheer volume of opportunity that is meaningful to everyone in the world we live in today.

Part of this 'culture creation' and rate of change is the pace of constant learning to allow for this to happen. The industry is challenged by many factors and driving towards this open culture that will foster true diversity of thought and therefore constant innovation, is something that challenges everyone. A huge step towards this can be seen in the success of people-to-people networking within the FinTech and financial services space. Mutual learning across the industry and between various professional groups has been a major component within this space that has allowed for the culture of open discussion, improvement, and innovation.

Eleni Vlami, the Head of Account Management at Meniga and another award-winning Woman of FinTech Powerlistee, said that these groups 'are triggering people to have a conversation and it's this networking where you can meet people and leverage abilities, share your knowledge, talk with each other and its helped me as an individual to grow'. Meniga is headquartered in Iceland and specialises in using transactional data better and prides itself in creating data-driven ecosystems for people, banks, and businesses. As Eleni points out, networking has become a huge part of how individuals grow within the industry and Anna Burgess, Senior Service Delivery Manager at Close Brothers, agrees. Anna said, 'networking is a really important part of building your career and people often underestimate it'. In her podcast she spoke about her experience working in Close Brothers, the merchant bank, and how important it is to realise that networking is both operational and strategic. She described how it will simply help you get things executed or will allow you to progress your career through advertising your skills and interests. She said 'we often think networking is personal and social' instead it allows one to learn, progress, and build upon their career through meaningful relationship building. For me networking has been about building professional relationships across the scope of the marketplace to gain insight, opinion and learn from the people 'walking the talk'.

My work for inclusion has been based on the concept of paying it forward where if I can add value to someone they will want to reciprocate. The membership economy of my network is rooted in an empathetic starting point where we can build towards a better workplace where we are more successful because of inclusion.

The harsh reality of what networking can be like for women is highlighted by Johanna Maria Leiner, the VP of Compliance, Governance and Ethics at Paysafe. Where women have been the minority in the room, often these networks are difficult to infiltrate, they take place in the evenings and have been described as boys clubs of like-minded thinking. Paysafe provides simple and secure payment solutions to businesses of all sizes around the world and Johanna runs many networking groups and meetings virtually and in person to advocate change. She says networking is a tremendous opportunity for women in the workplace as one of its aspects is about business introductions. We need to 'learn how to network, men are traditionally strong at asking for introductions, women should progress themselves through their networks, be your own fan - there will never be anyone who tells you how great you are, so stop waiting for it and tell yourself'.

The pandemic has allowed for further innovation in networking. Meet-ups were once held in pubs after working hours, right at the time parents put their children to bed. With the rise of working from home and being in lockdown we have been forced to try new ways of reaching out to one another. Webinars began with ferocity the minute the pandemic hit but the numbers of attendees did dwindle as meeting new people proved difficult though a 'videos off' zoom meeting.

We have seen a steady rise in creative ways to allow the power of networking to flourish. For me, I wanted to remind myself of the beauty of networking and it was something that Dr. Wajeeha H. Awadh, the Chief Digital Officer at the Al Baraka Banking Group, said that stood out. She felt that speaking in conferences, the telling of stories, the mutual learning, and the widening of one's network has a huge effect. 'It's an amazing feeling when you make an impact, speaking has a great and powerful influence on people and supporting and mentoring and speaking in conferences show us there are role models in the area and it does encourage more women to get into FinTech and that there are great opportunities here'. The learning isn't just internal to the industry, the strength of it is impacting those outside the industry and allowing them to affect change within it too. I met Dr Wajeeha at an EWPN event in Amsterdam in 2018 where she was able to share with me some of her achievements including being listed as one of the Most Influential Women in Islamic Business and Finance by Cambridge IFA.

Based in Bahrain she is passionate about changing the perceptions of what is possible in the industry, for women in particular and sees it as her responsibility to inspire others. It's this sentiment that drove me to run a number of campaigns under the banner of 'networking better' during our UK lockdowns of 2020 and 2021. Driven by the desire to inspire change, change perceptions, and to make action happen I began running roundtable series discussing a range of topics. I wanted to drive action through the sharing of knowledge and conversations between industry leaders, especially since I was seeing the UK government do so little to support women during the pandemic. Naturally one of the topics addressed the UK government's abolition of the gender pay gap as one of their first responses to the COVID-19 pandemic. I wanted to recreate the pre- and post-event coffee talks of face-to-face networking sessions and inspired by Wajeeha felt that we could improve this. My roundtables allowed for deeper relationships and more than just a five-minute hello before a talk, they allowed for the event to be the discussion itself, and furthermore I kept the groups small and intimate and created a series of follow-up events. This has created far better conversations, openness, honesty, and trust across the industry where people have shared their experiences and policies across firms to truly propel the industry forward. In webinars I have attended we are seeing the 'networking better' become apparent with the introduction of breakout rooms to encourage 3 or 4 people to take the conversation to the next level. We have seen panel conversations debate hot topics then each of the panellists speak directly with a select few of the audience to further collaboration and follow-up.

For diversity of thought and the successful debate to become a reality there is much learning to be done. For there to be gender equality in this sector there is even more work to be done. Tribeni Chougule, the Head of Change Management at Visa, described our current situation, 'there is a real call to action - the industry is focussing on it, but we shouldn't be under any illusion that there is a steep hill, in fact, a mountain to climb'. This mountain will need for us all to be willing to change, learn, and adapt. For gender equality to be reached and then for it to work we need some of these themes I've discussed to be part of the everyday DNA of firms within the FinTech community. Rebecca Duckworth spoke passionately about it in her podcast with me highlighting that 'we need fast and often communication, and we must make sure people have their inputs, whoever they are and wherever they are from'. Rebecca is the Chief Sales and Marketing Officer of QV Systems, a business dedicated to digitising asset and automotive finance. Yet another person dedicated to change for good and improving the status quo.

We have to be clear on what the status quo is right now for gender equality within the space and I wish to share some facts on how men in FinTech are being supported through funding and how women haven't been. We have looked at the statistics of the gender imbalance in the sector and we have seen the potential scale of the sector. According to Deloitte's Insights report published in late 2020 it is really clear that we have a huge funding gap in FinTech. Of the global FinTech Founder community, women account for only 7%. Interestingly, in 2010 FinTechs with women only founding teams and FinTechs with at least one woman on their founding team accounted for 10.9% of total start-ups. In 2019 this percentage had grown meagrely to 12.2%. Another find is that women-founded FinTechs have raised only one per cent of total FinTech investment across 2010–2019.

Talking about the gender imbalance itself is on the agenda, but the actions that are needed will have to make more of an impact than we have made in the past decade. The challenge of the COVID-19 pandemic is a huge topic I will be addressing later as an opportunity for us to make change happen despite how it has hindered women in the wider workplace. Liza Russell, the Chief Operating Officer of Inbotiqa, a next-generation Intelligent Business Email platform, says 'as women, look at what we are juggling and how many plates are we are spinning, we should be in those boardrooms talking about strategies for recovery because it's in our make-up, it's what we do'. We will be unveiling how there can be more of a balance in FinTech boardrooms, how we can ensure that every voice is heard and how every person with their diversity of thought can contribute.

There are so many other exciting topics that are relevant to FinTech and will pose challenges ripe to be overcome by the industry. We have Brexit, Open Finance, digital adoption, further value adds to customers and the education of the next generations to name a few. The list is endless, especially when we look at these topics through the looking glass of the 'FinTech Mindset' and the desire to turn any problem into an opportunity. Before delving into the 'hows' we need to briefly look at the change in technology and the tradition of institutional finance to really see the current landscape and barriers we must overcome in our drive towards workplace gender equality.

4

The Past: Traditional Financial Services and Technology Culture

To authentically tackle the gender imbalance within today's FinTech community, we must be clear about the history of exclusion in both finance and technology workplaces. In particular, I want to outline exactly which of the issues need to be addressed. We now know some of the figures, but how did we get here? What are the real problems we need to solve? How do we get to the root of making change happen?

There has been a tumultuous past of technology and diversity. We have seen this quite famously from the big scandals of Uber's Chief Executive Officer, having to exit the business in 2017 to the devastating admissions from YouTube's very own Chief Executive Officer, Susan Wojcicki, about her struggles for equality. Uber has been one of the big technology success stories to date, boasting huge advances for the transportation industry at a meteoric level. The reality was that behind closed doors the company had a toxic 'bro culture' that excluded women, discriminated against women, and had numerous allegations of sexual harassment. This was so severe that the Chief Executive Officer, Travis Kalanick, was forced to resign by the investors. Google, another technology monolith hit the headlines in 2017 when one of its former employees, published a 10-page anti-diversity memo insisting that women were less suited than men for roles within technology. I put it blandly, as in reality the memo was misogynistic, derogatory, and inflammatory about women's abilities to code for Google. The memo got out and went public. The 16th employee of Google, the Chief Executive Officer of YouTube, a Google-owned company, Susan Wojcicki, responded by saying 'I've had my

© The Author(s), under exclusive license to Springer Nature Switzerland AG 2022
N. Edwards-Dashti, *FinTech Women Walk the Talk*,
https://doi.org/10.1007/978-3-030-90574-3_4

abilities and commitment to my job questioned. I've been left out of key industry events and social gatherings. I've had meetings with external leaders where they primarily addressed the more junior male colleagues. I've had my comments frequently interrupted, and my ideas ignored until they were rephrased by men. No matter how often this all happened, it still hurt'. She went on to admit this memo could and would probably discourage women from joining the industry.

Of course, the question loomed for women in businesses worldwide, that if the Chief Executive Officer of one of the biggest technology giants the world has ever seen, feels this way then what hope do the rest of us have?

The overtly misogynistic culture of the gaming world has also added to the bad image of technology. This has included rape fantasies, glorification of domestic violence, and similar such barbarities that would never encourage a woman to feel welcome, let alone an equal member. Evidence has been reported that giants such as Amazon have used Artificial Intelligence software to allow them to automatically reject certain demographics from their job application processes. It doesn't take much to just imagine who these excluded groups may be. Even though everything you read is that these such practices have been shut down it does nothing to attract women to the industry. I have barely scratched the surface; we know the list goes on and on.

The investors of Uber persuaded Travis Kalanick to resign because they knew these practices were bad for business let alone their ethics. Google sacked the ignoramus who wrote the anti-diversity memo because again, imagine if 50% of the world's computer literate population moved from using Google to Yahoo? I am spurned on by other investors making this decision. I believe together this change will be made to happen so we can have equals within business no matter their gender, culture, creed, age, class etc., for the good of society and for the good of our businesses.

As a history graduate, I am extremely drawn to the past and understanding why things are the way they are. I am very much conscious for us not to repeat the same mistakes and one of the recurring themes of the gender imbalance problem is when businesses or their leaders try to paper over the cracks of their issues.

It has become so obvious that there are huge voids in the old exclusive ways of thinking. The exciting change to the narrative is driven by the women I have been celebrating. A great example of this is Billie Simmons, who taught me about how she is bridging some of those gaps by empowering and bettering her community. She said that when she was 'training as a software engineer, that was the first time I felt I had tangible skills that could improve the lives of LGBTQ+ people'.

Billie is the Co-Founder of Daylight, the first and only digital banking platform in the US specifically designed for and by the LGBTQ+ community. She spoke about how much opportunity there is in the industry if only you can look at it from your own unique perspective. When talking about who the financial systems of today are built for, she said 'finance was built for and by straight, white, cis men. When you look through that lens it suddenly makes sense. For example, it's super hard to change your name legally, what it does to your credit score, your banking systems and processes involved - who is the one group of people who by and large never have to change their name? Straight, white, cis men'. She concluded, 'the system wasn't built for us'. There are thousands upon thousands of gaps out there that the old system simply won't have any idea about.

Anna Flach, Global Marketing Director for BSO, a leading infrastructure and connectivity provider for financial markets, talks about what she has seen in her years of working within the industry and says, 'there are way too many gaps we hear about; the gender pay gap, the gender funding gap, the gender investment gap, why is that?' She went on to say there is a gender confidence gap and gender leadership gap, all of which we need to find the cause of, to be able to solve these problems. She was clear when she said, 'I just don't believe that women are less capable or less ambitious than men, I think there are other factors playing a part and it doesn't make any sense given that we are fighting a war for talent. It would be really good to tap into the other 50% so there is a real business case for' a better gender balance. It's these 'gaps' that we have to tackle to truly make the desired change happen, and these gaps are bigger than the HR department of one firm to fix. They are societal, political, governmental and all of these gaps need every single person in the workplace to attempt to wrestle for real change to take place.

Looking at the gender pay gap here in the UK there is still much work to be done. Following the Equality Act of 2010, the UK finally introduced gender pay gap reporting, a yawning seven years later in 2017. This meant that across all UK companies of 250 people or larger now had to submit data on their gender balance and statistics on how they were paying their men and women. This raising of awareness and transparency has helped ensure more organisations are taking steps to tackle inequality at work, but more action is needed. As of 2019 the gender pay gap remained stubbornly high at 17.3% meaning that for every pound men were earning, their female counterparts were taking home 83p for doing the same job. This pay gap is similar to where it was in 2017 at 17.9% when reporting started.

The Charted Institute for Personnel and Development reported that the reasons for the gap were complex. They are clear to highlight the difference between unequal pay and the gender pay gap. The gap itself is not just about the reporting of basic salaries, which is termed unequal pay, it's about a pay gap which has a number of elements that can affect it. These elements include workplace provision of childcare, flexibility on hours, reporting lines, and expectation of presenteeism, amongst other things, all of which have been typically considered when deciding on pay. These have been true for the way bonuses are allocated as well as the way promotions are decided upon. Other factors include women being the main providers of unpaid caring responsibilities at home, the way men and women ask for more money and how men and women's work is perceived in the workplace.

Research has found that there currently exists a 'motherhood penalty', where working mothers face disadvantages in the workplace with regard to perceptions of their competence, dedication, and aspirations. It's these perceptions that we hear about again and again where women are having to deal with challenges men simply don't. When applying for roles as a woman, Sangeetha Narasimham says, 'even before your CV has got to the table there are barriers to break'. Sangeetha is the Director of Global Acquisition Marketing at Mambu, a cloud banking platform that empowers their customers to build and change banking products easily. In conversations with me she spoke about the need to break down these barriers of perception and tradition to really be able to affect change.

Sylvia Carrasco agreed and said in her podcast, 'I don't like playing the victim, but I still appreciate that women have probably a harder task than men. We have to prove ourselves more than men and that in itself is a challenge'. The Founder and Chief Executive Officer of GoldEx, the first gold marketplace powered by smart technology, went on to say 'I have never met a woman in the FinTech space who isn't very strong and very capable'. Regardless of strength and capability, one of the key factors in the identification of these gaps is about levelling the playing field to make the system fairer and more equitable for everyone.

Women have not been given the same opportunities to be within businesses, to progress and to stay. We see that clearly in the numbers we have looked at and the few stories of the technology world that I have shared. Anna Flach of BSO also questioned why women at schools and universities outperform their male counterparts and continue to do so into their twenties at work, but then what happens after thirty? The 'motherhood penalty' both perceived and real in terms of time taken out of careers has certainly affected progression. The sustainability of someone being able to work like they did in their twenties without the responsibility of aged parents and young children also plays a part. As do responsibilities that often lie on the shoulders of women because of systemic problems we see in society and lack of government support.

During the COVID-19 pandemic we saw the UK government let down women again and again. As mentioned, one of their first responses to the pandemic was to abandon the gander pay gap for 2020, just weeks before the numbers were due to be submitted. We saw unprecedented numbers of women lose their jobs and others made the 'choice' to resign from jobs to deal with the childcare of their household whilst schools were closed. In fact, women were the majority of workers put on furlough across the UK in March—August 2020. Roughly 133,000 more women were furloughed than men across the UK. Thinking again at how the government produced sexist adverts for the population to 'stay at home' to stay safe from the virus and depicted images of women at home cleaning, caring, and cooking. Naturally they retracted such images quickly releasing statements no one believed saying 'this is not our view of women'. What surprised me was how such an advert had made it to the press. Had it not been seen by one woman? Who surely would have noticed zero representation of the working woman, and pointed it out, or perhaps it had been signed off by women who simply didn't feel they could point out the transgression?

The history of women in the banking world isn't dissimilar to the bad press of the technology giants we looked at earlier. In the 2010s, following the aftermath of the 2008 recession brought on by the banks over lending mortgages, there was so much to read in the newspapers about where and how the banks had got it 'all wrong'. As part of the widespread 'bank bashing' there was much to learn about the female experience. It was easy to see examples such as the one where in 1972, where a question on an entrance exam paper for a trainee programme at the Bank Merrill Lynch read, 'when you meet a woman, what interests you most about her?' This unacceptable question by today's standards, however many years later, does little for the image of finance. Banks have struggled to get it 'right' and so many still do. Over the years, in podcasts and conversations with people who work in the financial institutions I have gathered lots of evidence I won't be able to quote. Using the gender pay gap as an example, Banks generally have a higher proportion of women in their lower paying roles and lesser proportion in their higher paying roles. Simply put, the world of finance has traditionally struggled to retain their women in jobs, invest in the growth of those women, or promote those women. Going back to my point on the perceived and real 'motherhood penalty' it's important to note that it's the very easy answer to say that women drop off because of motherhood. And to answer Anna's question of what happens to these women in their thirties, I haven't seen that women have left their roles in financial institutions because they wanted to raise children. In fact, I've seen women move out of banking to set up their own firms, join FinTech start-ups, apply for funding, join vendors and exchanges before embarking on their maternity journey. Some have left their roles to raise children, but this isn't the majority and it is true to say a huge proportion has left the industry altogether.

The biggest problems cited were around pay, promotion, and credit. These three points I will raise and raise again throughout this book. They are all about value and perceived value and where Susan Wojckicki spoke about not being heard in meetings until male counterparts had rephrased her points and taken credit, this is similar to the experience for so many women across the finance space and I'm sure across all workplaces. Giving credit to the right person for an idea, for the work, for making something happen, is hugely important to morale. Its inextricably linked to confidence and self-worth. The female experience as I plan to showcase is very much littered with crises of confidence, questioning of one's ability, and the dreaded 'imposter syndrome' where you start to believe you aren't competent in what you do. This confidence gap isn't relevant to all women but is certainly a factor for many. None of this is a surprise if we see that women are valued less through their pay, valued less through their titles, let alone the lack of recognition of their progression and valued less every single day when credit is attributed elsewhere. The importance of networking cannot but underestimated here as traditionally networking was drinks in the pub which relied upon who was invited. Typically women were less so and they remained in the office quietly stacking up their hours, ideas, input without the recognition, pat on the back, or the all-important popularity vote. This vote of popularity or vote of confidence is often a passing comment or head nod when names are put forward for promotion. This has happened far less for these women and they go on without recognition or credit. With all this in mind, it's no wonder that by the time women have given ten years of their career to this type of environment they become disillusioned and want out. Perhaps we should re-think the sweeping generalisations blaming motherhood for exits. When we lose women from our businesses, it is not always out of our control because they wanted to have children, so we shouldn't write it off as something we can't do anything about. Once we stop finger-pointing at the women as the reasons why we have a gender imbalance and look at what we can change in the systems and ourselves, then the real work can begin.

Over half a century on from the 1972 question (where beauty was the correct answer by the way) most Banks will have Diversity and Inclusion

Heads of Department employed to tackle the problem of the gender imbalance. These banks will have diversity quotas they wish to hit when hiring and some will even have Diversity and Inclusion think tanks set up to brainstorm what can be done. These Diversity and Inclusion heads will be remitted to ensure discrimination doesn't take place, that everyone's voices are heard and even though a minority, women are able to lead teams without being undermined or personally attacked. Even with these new roles in place the problem remains.

When I was interviewing George Coxon, the Chief Operating Officer of Nano Foundation, she was open about her thoughts and really brought this point home in today's context. Nano Foundation is a Foundation on a mission to truly 'democratise money, creating an economy that is free and open to all'. She shared, 'the barriers I have personally faced have been tough over the past three years in the crypto currency space I think it's important to delineate between the two different facets here. There is sexism that exists in the professional sector of blockchain and then there's sexism that exists in the rhetoric of internet trolls who profit off the unaccountability of the internet'. She went on to speak about the gender gaps including the investment gap and wider societal changes that are needed to affect the industry. When describing her own purpose, she explained how her cryptocurrency not-for-profit is about making money 'accessible and open to all'. In doing that she said, 'the inclusivity of women is an absolute must! How can we exclude half the world's population when creating a global currency?' a point I think we can all agree with and must commit to making happen. Open to all really means that, and she is on a mission to close these gaps.

Dagmara Aldridge, the Chief Operating Officer of Zumo, highlighted yet another gap, one she calls the 'disparity gap' in how men and women are given feedback. Zumo is a Crypto Currency firm striving to make the world of digital currencies more accessible and a trusted currency. She spoke in depth about her research and years of experience highlighting that feedback for women in the workplace is often 'less actionable and less effective' compared to that given to men, in their reviews. In developmental conversations for women managers feedback 'tends to focus on delivery rather than vision, coping with politics, rather than leveraging politics, and collaboration rather than assertiveness' all holding back the individual in question. We discussed at length the damaging notion of 'coping with politics' as a solution for women in the workplace rather than 'leveraging' or providing solutions to the politics women face. Dagmara's passion for progressing people to their true potential means that this is a particular problem that she wishes to solve saying 'we must provide tools and design processes that ensure that feedback inconsistency between genders no longer exists and we have a level-playing field to excel'. Awareness is the crucial first step that is needed here for people to identify their own behaviours in management before they can learn how to improve and change their behaviours.

To draw upon Anna Flach's podcast yet again, she said, 'I've never been treated differently, and I had the same opportunities as my brother - but I have still noticed differences having joined the world of work and some barriers. For instance, having worked in investment backing it is true that there are more men than women, especially in senior positions and sometimes you do get that feeling of boys' club decision making'. This feeling of exclusion and struggle to reach the inner circle isn't one where she is alone. This has been a theme that recurred through my many conversations with women across the sector. It's often the feeling that your opinions are not heard, or your suggestions are ignored and this gets exhausting further contributing to the confidence gap.

In talks with Erin Taylor, the Founder of Finthropology, she shared a recent report she and Anette Broløs had produced for the European Women's Payment Network. Finthropology is a research and consulting firm, and the report was called Female Finance in Figures: an EWPN report examining the characteristics of 102 organisations offering financial services to women. Within this Erin and Anette showcased the rising number of 'financial products and investments apps designed specifically for women' each with the social goal of trying to narrow the financial gender gap through providing women with financial services that respond to their real-life needs. Unlike Anna's experience, Erin highlighted that the norm is more 'often brothers receive more financial education than their sisters, there is already a disadvantage for women from a young age'. This further hinders women in their ability to do well financially, their desire to join the industry, and their belief in becoming a success within it. Businesses are beginning to see the opportunities in serving the underserved and we should all play our part in the education of our youngsters to stop this particular cycle.

Because finance was so traditionally male-dominated and often made up of certain men educated in similar ways, from the same class, and having lived similar experiences growing up, there is a hangover of the behaviours that worked and were acceptable then, that continue now. We are as a society learning that differences of opinions make us stronger, different perspectives make us better, and encouraging these viewpoints is key to a successful business. However, as many managers have said to me 'old habits die hard'. Ritesh Jain is a leader within the financial services and FinTech space. His career has spanned over 20 years where he has led teams in firms like Visa in payments,

Mearsk in logistics and the well-known bank HSBC. He has now founded his own business Infynit, on a mission to 'humanise credit and credit cards'. In his years of working, he has seen so many environments that abide by this old way of decision-making known as 'group think'. He says, 'as a leader you shouldn't be building followers but building leaders free to discuss their own insights'. He introduced me to the concept of not allowing a HiPPO to take over your meetings, which stands for 'Highest Paid persons opinion'. He was incredibly insightful in explaining to me something that I now recognise is the experience of so many others. This being the board, management, or team meeting where decisions must be made and the culture in that room is to hold in one's own thoughts so not to disagree with the highest paid person in the room. Meetings and decision-making have been thwarted for years with this problem and the problem goes beyond that one person. My experience of 'group think' has been to be told endless examples where the majority in the room tend to think the same, have lived similar experiences, face the same challenges, and perceive the world from similar viewpoints. As a minority in that room it's often incredibly hard to find the space let alone the reception to provide that alternative viewpoint. People and their lived experience are often overlooked, not seen as significant, or denied, in favour of doing things the way they have always been done. It's easier that way, it's not unknown, it's in peoples comfort zones to agree and carry on as normal, therefore it's also easy to see the perpetrator of thinking differently as the 'difficult' one. 'Group think' has been apparent for many years and was an acceptable way of doing business until the onset of innovation and change in the industry. Having been so prevalent it makes raising awareness so much more important.

With all of this in mind it's no wonder that Maya Aweida once said to me that, 'FinTechs have even less of a chance' when we discussed how the industry needs to affect change. When we spoke, Maya was part of the founding team at FinTech start-up HUBX, a platform built to ease the process for founders and financial professionals to raise capital. She spoke about these low levels of diversity in both technology and finance and was quick to raise the point that if FinTechs wish to build their businesses by hiring people only from each of these sectors they will simply perpetuate the problem of gender imbalance and all the gaps that appear alongside it.

The funding gap is a huge barrier for FinTechs to 'stand a chance' of being able to drive change. Sara Green Brodersen agreed and touched upon the lack of awareness men in finance and technology can have of the problem. Sara has built many businesses from scratch over her entire career starting her first at the age of 16. Since then, she's started two more companies, including FinTech Canaree and ID verification tool Deemly. She highlighted that male founders in FinTech often 'don't see the problem that women face' when it comes to funding and quoted Deloitte who published a report in 2020, that found 'women-founded FinTech's raised an average of 50% less capital over the past five years than start-ups founded only by men'. She has persisted and continually raises the topic with her male counterparts, because she believes the strength of inclusion is about including everybody to make us all better in our businesses.

In talking with Randa Bennett, another female founder, she shared a similar vein saying, 'the real world is men and women'. Randa is a second time Founder and CEO of vHelp, a payment solution for the third sector. She is incredibly passionate about 'competing in the real world' of business and having raised funding a couple of times she said, 'raising money is a very difficult thing whether you are male or female'. Her story was an insightful one as she shared so openly how she felt about the numerous pitches she and her co-founder did. She described the experience as 'disheartening' especially knowing about the dire funding gap statistics, but they persevered. Her feedback is clear and actionable advice for women pitching their business to investors today. 'One of the first questions you get asked about when raising money is how much traction do you have? How many users? How many clients?' She felt that once she was able to evidence their traction, she began to make headway. She rationalises this by saying 'people want to see more traction before they put in money because that reduces the risk for them' and in conclusion she felt if you had a good product, you were bringing on new clients and could evidence it, then investment would follow. In addressing some of these gaps throughout the book I want to share the advice that the 'women of FinTech' have imparted in their podcasts with me.

Interestingly another Founder, Caroline Hughes spoke of a similar experience but with slightly different opinion on it. Caroline is the Chief Executive Officer of the award-winning FinTech, Lifetise, a company which seeks to financially empower the masses by helping people better understand how to save, spend, and manage their money. When talking of her experience she said as women we know 'we get funded less often and with less money' and stated that 'men get funded and promoted on potential and women get promoted and funded once we have already proved that we have got that traction'. An interesting point is that both women, alongside many others, have used the word traction with me. Caroline compared the funding gap, with the promotion gap and then with the investment gap too. She said that looking at the facts, women 'are often better stewards of companies and we often get better returns' so for her one of her goals is to solve the problem by becoming an angel investor herself in the future. She was disappointed to see that 'group think' in investment was meaning that amazing business ideas were not getting the backing they deserved because the 'same type of people are getting funded'. A point we must sit up and take note of.

Thankfully there are many people and firms who identify these gaps and put action in place to address them. Continuing the funding gap issue I want to draw upon the podcast I recorded with Marta Zaccagnini, Program Manager for Europe at Village Capital, the largest supporter of impact-driven seed-stage start-ups in the world. Village Capital designs ways to mitigate bias in the funding processes by, as Marta describes, 'being purpose driven to create an ecosystem that works together allowing us to work with entrepreneurs with lived experience to build better products to solve problems'. Their model is based on the novel idea of peer selection where they aim to break down barriers for entrepreneurs and ensure that overlooked ideas are given weight. 'Peer selection aims to change this power dynamic' in funding where we see 'group think' still playing its part. The results are clear, changing the way funding works.

Village Capital's associated venture capital fund, VilCap Investments, has invested in over 110 peer-selected programme participants. More than 40% of the companies in the portfolio are female-led. As I will repeatedly say, changing the power dynamics will change the results, if only we are as agile as we say we are.

Another great example of challenging this 'group think' began in 2008, when Vanessa Vallely OBE started up WeAreTheCity community to 'inform women about things they can do for themselves in terms of driving their own careers' and later their sister site WeAreTechWomen to allow women to network freely with one another and learn from one another. Vanessa, having had 25 years' worth of a career in Banking, holding roles such as Head of Governance, Business Management, and Chief Operating Officer across nine financial institutions, remembers, 'back in 2008 gender wasn't on anyone's agenda really, diversity wasn't even a term, there wasn't much going on for women, in fact there wasn't much going on for anyone because it was recession'. Despite the strain the recession was putting on the City and the world of finance at the time Vanessa wanted to change the status quo and in turn has created much bigger change for women in the years that followed. To name just a few of the successes in the years 2015–2020, 950 women from over 25 sectors have been recognised through her Rising Star and TechWomen100 awards. Through WeAreTheCity and WeAreTechWomen's conferences and events, Vanessa and her team have helped to upskill over 12,000 women.

Again, changing how we tackle the problem will change the results. What we don't do when addressing the issues is look at these gaps clearly enough.

I have only touched the tip of the iceberg on them but it's not enough. We need to ask ourselves what do these gaps really mean for women working in finance or technology or FinTech? Chief Executive Officers of businesses don't ask themselves this question enough. I ask you would you want to do it? Would you want to battle and be the minority every day?

Tackling this together is paramount. It can't be on one minority demographic to change the system. I will say again we all have to look at this together and change together, not one department but all of us throughout the industries we exist in, should we wish to have the courage to make real change happen.

5

Change: Technology, Transformation, and Communication

We know that change needs to happen. Change in our environments, change in our systems, and change in our behaviours. We cannot expect one team within a business to enforce this change and we cannot expect to put this on any one minority. Change for all will need involvement from all of us.

It's pretty good timing that we are currently living in the fourth industrial revolution of large-scale change for all of humankind. It was a number of the 'Women of FinTech' who drew my attention to the sheer potential change dynamic we were living in. My inner historian kicked in and I looked back in history. I read about the colossal change that took place in the first industrial revolution, where water and steam mechanised production in turn completely changing the lives of people worldwide. Then again, what change took place in the second industrial revolution, with electricity allowing for mass production. It is quite awe inspiring to think about how lives were lived before each of the mammoth changes to industry and therefore society. The third industrial revolution is much more relatable, and some of us remember the onset of electronics and technology being used to automate how things are produced. We often can forget how much change we as human beings are capable of. It is this that's in my mind when I think about the goal of parity in the workplace. It isn't a huge task when you think of the farmers of the 1700s using their sickles in their fields alongside horse-drawn carts who left the only world they knew to travel to the 'big' cities to work in mechanised factories.

© The Author(s), under exclusive license to Springer Nature Switzerland AG 2022
N. Edwards-Dashti, *FinTech Women Walk the Talk*,
https://doi.org/10.1007/978-3-030-90574-3_5

The fourth industrial revolution is about building on the third and digitalising technology. We are seeing this every day in the financial services industry and FinTech world through Blockchain, Artificial Intelligence, Big Data, Robotics, Nanotechnology, and so much more. The smart phone phenomenon, the way we do our banking, the digitalisation of cash, the targeting of the 'unbanked', these are all things that are changing every industry, every sector, every person worldwide. Furthermore, as with each previous industrial revolution we have seen vast societal improvements. We have seen them worldwide, in how we live our lives, in accessing people living in poverty in ways we couldn't have imagined possible, in supplying cities with food or water where we struggled to previously, in giving people the opportunity to work without relying on location as a factor for employment. Whilst there are many positives, there is also scope for the advancement in technology to increase the gap between the rich and the poor worldwide. Some worry these advancements will simply make the rich richer.

This is why it is so important that we are seeing the rise of FinTechs with missions and purposes greater than that of financial institutions of bygone eras. Missions based on financial inclusion, serving those who were previously 'underserved', green finance and those who support environmentally friendly causes are certainly on the rise.

The perfect example of this comes from Kimberley Abbott, the Founder and Chief Executive Officer of a business called Vested, which measures meaningful impact across businesses. An engineer by background with experience working for the UN, Kimberley has dedicated her company to solve how we measure Environmental, Societal, and Corporate Governance impact. And how an organisation actually contributes to society's biggest challenges. She says, 'money itself doesn't change the world, it's the people that spend it that do' and 'if we don't change finance, we won't finance change'. She talks about solving problems from poverty to climate change and 'If you want to change the world you have to deal with the levers in power'. Powerful words which really shine the appropriate light on the inclusion mission we are on.

This fourth industrial revolution is changing everyone's lives and the concept of working in or studying Science, Technology, Engineering, or Mathematics or STEM as it is often referred to is becoming more mainstream. We are seeing a departure from the derogatory verbiage of 'nerd' or 'geek' when describing technologists, as so many of us are using technology in increasing facets of our lives.

I loved listening to Evgenia Loginova, the Co-Founder and Chief Executive Officer of Radar Payments, say 'everything we do in life is going to be more and more digitalised so working in technology shouldn't be a scary proposition'. Evgenia shared her journey to Chief Executive Officer in her podcast with such clarity. Telling us about Radar Payments and what they do differently as a payment services provider and how the underlying complexities of their work shouldn't be perceived as a drawback for female talent. She was adamant about moving away from the perception women have that technology is clinical, dispassionate, and all about coding. In her view, math and science are not male topics and we should start bringing that message to women early on when they make choices about what to study next. The next wave of technology, she mentioned, hinting at AI, data, and ecosystems, will need a lot of skills around collaboration, ethics, and transparency that in all fairness fit very well with what she described as feminine skills and leadership styles. She spoke of how, having studied art or history, women should pursue FinTech, as there are plenty of options for their training and cited how many women she had seen who had successfully made that transition. Taking me back to the mission, the purpose, and the drivers of companies in FinTech; technology is the vehicle, and we need to enlighten ourselves about the journey.

These preconceptions we see around technology are largely perpetuated by what we deem as technology and it is paramount that we all play our part in dispelling these myths. OakNorth has been heralded as the UK's fastest-growing FinTech and its purpose is to build the future of commercial lending for growth businesses to allow them to scale. Valentina Kristensen is their Director of Growth and Communications, and has driven their hypergrowth since 2016. She shines a light on this topic by saying 'It's a misconception that working in STEM means you are in a lab coat or sitting at a computer coding'. She went on to list the positions in OakNorth that she would class as working in STEM because they are within the ecosystem of a FinTech. She spoke of compliance, business development, operation, marketing, sales, and all because each are 'all hugely important roles which make the company grow'. 'Without them', she continued 'it doesn't matter what the coders might be doing because if there's no one to sell or market the product then it's a bit of a wasted effort'.

Interestingly when I spoke with Andrea Sparke the Managing Director and Head of Sales of Toppan Merrill she continued on this thread. She spoke about her own acceptance that she is a woman of STEM. She conceded that 'its taken me years to even think STEM is in my space which is crazy! We need to show what a great industry it is to be part of, forward looking, forward thinking but importantly with a heart'. Toppan Merrill is a leader in financial printing and communication solutions and boasts its commitment to better customer experience. Andrea's background as an expert within the

Financial Printing space, Banking, and Politics, she believes means she can bring a wealth of ability to ensuring she brings a better customer experience every single day. She went on to say that there is 'a lot of creativity and the key is being inquisitive, finding like-minded mentors or leaders who you want to follow or join'.

Furthermore, the more podcasts I recorded the more I found myself saying 'and here we have another "woman of FinTech" who didn't study computer science'. I was and still am seeing Geography, Anthropology, English, and Philosophy degrees and sometimes no degrees at all as the starting points of many of the women's careers that we now see as senior, leaders, and C-level members of staff within the FinTech and financial services community. I want to celebrate that. Many companies still have the archaic prerequisite that upon job application that the applicant must have an 'Oxbridge' or 'Redbrick' degree. Throughout the past 17 years of my recruitment career, I have worked with thousands of people in the position to hire a new member of staff or 'hiring manager'. It has been a frequent demand that the only people they would deem 'good enough' for their team is someone who was able to garner a place on a STEM course at Oxford, Cambridge, or the other traditional universities founded in industrial cities in the nineteenth century now known as 'Redbrick'. The huge changes in technology and the onset of mission led businesses have meant that the hiring conversation has begun the move, albeit slowly, from whether someone is 'good enough' to whether they have the 'potential'. This is an incredibly exciting step for the world of work, the world of innovation and diversity of thought.

I will evidence all the work I have witnessed to attract more women to STEM subjects as young girls and the work with universities to attract a wider diversity of background to the financial services and FinTech community. So much can be celebrated here but there are two sides to this coin, attracting more talent to STEM and understanding that technology world has moved beyond STEM-only academics. I am a great believer in future technologists coming from a variety of backgrounds and in my everyday job of helping companies grow their technology teams and helping individuals build great career paths. This is a huge topic in which I am starting to see progress.

Since having the conversation with Andrea, I have asked many others if they consider themselves within STEM and more and more of the 'women of FinTech' with their variety of backgrounds have agreed that having thought about it, they do. It is this 'having thought about it' I wish to address in all of our minds. Technology is in everything we do so we must start seeing it as something we all have access to, rather than it being something 'over there' that other people do.

Let us for one moment just acknowledge the plethora of backgrounds we are seeing some of the greats within the industry coming from. Billie Simmons, the Co-Founder of Daylight, studied Pop Music at degree level. She sees this as a strength saying 'I can walk into this industry and see things that are broken and ask why are they broken? I don't have these internal biases that come with working in the banking industry your entire life'. Because of this enlightened way of thinking she is able to identify huge gaps in the financial world where there haven't been specific products delivering to needs of the LGBTQ+ community and just as importantly, where there hasn't been the access.

George Coxon, the Chief Operating Officer of Nano Foundation studied Anthropology, and because of her background is so passionate about including all saying, 'an economy that is open to all and that empowers all those that are marginalised, and that's not only financially but socially and politically, will be more robust and resilient'. Similarly, Katharine Wooller, the Managing Director of Dacxi, having studied History, attributes her way of utilising technology to her days at Cambridge. She believes 'if you put the customer first, you can build a very strong business, and technology is a very good means to that end'. Another powerful woman in STEM who isn't a Technologist but instead very good at explaining what technology can do for a customer. Having scaled a business in the peer-to-peer and investment world from 4 to over 1000 people she believes you have to be incredibly customer focused. She was also able to proudly say that her Crypto Wealth Platform business has a gender balance of 55% who identify as female and says she has achieved this by going for the best candidate for the role and breaking down the barriers of what is possible with regard to flexibility.

When I spoke with Cindy van Niekerk, she recalled her first days upon entering the industry. She reminisced, 'I studied in Travel and Tourism, and someone took a chance on me!' She went on to say that she has no idea about the finance industry when she started working within it, but once she understood it, she was able to specialise in regulation. Cindy is now Founder and Chief Executive Officer of Umazi, a business dedicated to allowing corporations to create a single digital identity to share across industries automating due diligence in real-time.

Each is passionate about showing that the technology industry can be made up of people from different backgrounds as they themselves have shown. Alia Cooper, EMEA Head of Compliance Framework for HSBC, tells of a similar story. 'I didn't take the direct route' she says and then continues to share how she studied Social Anthropology and discovered she had a talent for coding when was asked to do a favour for a colleague. Working a summer job at Manchester Computing Centre she was asked to help out with some coding and picked up a book and taught herself what to do. This opened up Alia's eyes to having a career in technology and she continued, 'I was in the unfortunate position because I hadn't done a technology degree and there weren't many organisations that were open to non-technology specialists joining technology roles'. It was British Airways who did give Alia the opportunity to learn their operational computer language when other firms chose not to, instead demanding technology degrees for their new joiners. This is a wonderful example of how anyone reading this can make a change right now about who they believe can be their next great teammate or hire. More importantly, the choices made by those in positions of hiring dictate the future and potential success of our entire industry. I see it as my responsibility to help these 'hiring managers' see this potential and feel more comfortable in investing in people for technology but without technology degrees.

Looking at what we define as technology roles today is so much more varied than what we considered technology roles back in 2010. As a recruiter, the decade of the 2010s saw huge advancements in the need for technologists to communicate. Not just to one another but to people who were not technologists and to people who were external to their team or business. From a skill set point of view, I have seen a huge growth of what I call 'hybrid roles', where hands-on coding skills are required alongside requirements gathering skills, typically associated with Business Analysts, those who analyse what needs to be achieved. Historically, where a Tester or Quality Assurance person would make sure the systems worked once they have been coded, I started seeing that this individual now needed to communicate any problems they ran in to and suggest improvements. There is a myriad of examples I could give here but the point is that technology, however technical it is, is now all about how that system build is communicated to those who requested its build. How that build can be done better, hurdles that need to be overcome, challenges along the way, and how all of this is explained to the ones who will be using it, buying it, or integrating it. Agile has become the standard way of working, where frequent communication and feedback across the team, throughout every step of a system build or 'sprint' is essential for constant improvements.

Seeing each of these new types of roles emerge alongside the new prominence of collaboration, discussion, evaluation, and debate has been such an exciting part of my job. As a non-technologist I have loved every minute of encouraging people to speak to me about how things work, how they are put together and the challenges they overcome. I've found it fascinating to learn so much and to be able to speak to so many diverse personality types with the new skill set that make up today's technologist.

Annette Evans, the Vice President of People and Culture at Global Processing Services, a payment processing partner, said 'what can we learn from technology? Let's incorporate agile methodologies into everything we do not just the technological sprints'. She spoke passionately about the people within GPS and how to ensure as a rapidly growing business they felt supported yet challenged, driven yet nurtured. Annette is the epitome of woman within FinTech using technology methodologies in her line of work to invest in her people and open up the opportunities for us all.

With so much change we really have a huge opportunity to make change happen for gender equality but there are certainly barriers we need to break, and these will be my next points of discussion.

6

Reality: The Issues We Must Acknowledge

To recognise how we might improve, I need to be clear about what the industry landscape looks and feels like for women in FinTech. We know we have a gender imbalance and we have reviewed some of the historic reasons as to why in previous chapters. This chapter is about us understanding the unique challenges any minority, and typically women, face day in, day out in their working environment. As I delve into this, I want us to ask the questions: why don't we attract more women to FinTech? Why don't more women stay in FinTech? What is it like to work in a male-dominated environment? When we hear about the systemic bias, that we must challenge and overcome, what exactly do we mean?

The best way for me to make sense of it is by reminding us of the famous quote by Alexander den Heijer, a Dutch inspirational speaker, trainer, and consultant; 'When a flower doesn't bloom, you fix the environment in which it grows, not the flower'.

For too long we have been looking at changing women in the hope for them to join the FinTech and financial services industries. I wish to outline the areas we could change should we wish to attract, retain, and promote more women to the space.

Much has been written about the UK technology sector and the challenges we face. We have looked at how in 2021 only 17% roles within technology are filled by women. When looking at FinTech specifically, the figures for women in the space are at 30% and when assessing the leadership within FinTech women make up 17% again. *The Guardian* newspapers have cited these

N. Edwards-Dashti, *FinTech Women Walk the Talk*,
https://doi.org/10.1007/978-3-030-90574-3_6

figures multiple times over the years, whilst recruitment international.com, PricewaterhouseCoopers, and hr.director.com state similar statistics.

We have seen so much data about the lack of funding and the limited numbers of women in FinTech, that we are almost numb to the rhetoric. And yet, to date, nothing has brought to life the negative impact of this day-to-day reality for those impacted, the women themselves. I wish to change that through sharing the experiences many women have shared with me personally in my engagements with them over the years.

Every business is different, every team is different, and every person has their own unique experience and perspective in any given event. What I will cite is the overwhelming narrative of commonplace barriers to change that I hear and see time and time again. It is necessary to acknowledge this to break down the blockers of equality. It is paramount to acknowledge the inextricable link these equality barriers have in limiting a company's true potential. Without achieving equality, we are impeding people, teams, and FinTech businesses from achieving all the success factors we discussed previously around diversity of thought, agility, ability to debate and problem solve at the highest level.

Until we have more senior women in a male-dominated industry, Caroline Hughes, Chief Executive Officer of Lifetise says 'it will remain difficult for new opinions and perspectives to break through'. To build financial services that work for everyone, we need leaders who 'have curiosity outside their own experience'. Without any curiosity we simply cannot build an industry where problems we didn't know existed are getting solved. She isn't alone when she recalls times where other business leaders have not wanted to hear the perspective or have ended a much-needed conversation. I have heard so many women share their experience of being overlooked, unheard, spoken over, interrupted or ignored in meetings and many have attributed these events to the demise of their own confidence and in turn their desire to speak up. When talking about the 'confidence gap' I often am reminded of these examples. Caroline is adamant that the 'confidence gap' in the industry isn't about women's confidence at all but instead it reflects the fact that women are often excluded from the decision-making parts of the system saying, 'It's about putting women into a system where they can't win - we must change the system'. Imagine that for a moment. The next time you put an idea forward that it's not seen as valuable by the majority of the room you are in, or even worse, that it is repeated by someone else and then agreed with instantly.

And yet, women are also expected to temper any innate confidence they may have or retain with more 'feminine' traits as empathy and altruism—merely 'acting like a man' with forthright displays of confidence and self-belief will do little to advance their careers.

When discussing change and becoming aware of new 'lived experiences' it makes sense that everyone must be curious. Everyone has to want to hear about someone else's perspective and experience to be able to cater to their demographic as a customer. When we have a system that is led by many who still subscribe to 'group think' or the perceived safety of 'echo chambers' we are unable to achieve real 'diversity of thought' and the superpower it can offer a business. 'Group think' and the behaviours associated with it are damaging to anyone who thinks differently. It is incredibly difficult to take any alternate notion forward in the realm of that environment. The word 'exhausting' has been used to describe this so many times. Exhausting to be ignored, exhausting to feel unheard, and exhausting to see others in the business be praised and valued for ideas that began as yours. In a world where I speak to so many leaders about ensuring your workforce is engaged and motivated, we are really holding ourselves back by not getting this right.

This is why I feel the correct attribution of credit at every stage of any outcome is so important. If we want to create environments where people feel encouraged to create, innovate, and strive for methods never used before, reward, recognition, respect, and praise have to be fair and equitable. It's not about the patronising pat on the back, it's about parity. It's not only about ideas in meetings either, but also about how that person is valued in the business. How that incumbent is then perceived by the team, how they are listened to or spoken to, and how they are then promoted.

Thea Fisher, a prominent leader within the FinTech space moved into the educational technology sector after 5 years. When she worked within the FinTech community she was a Commercial Manager for Littlepay, an international payments technology start-up and said, 'I do think that FinTech can appear quite unwelcoming for women and that doesn't necessarily mean that it is. I obviously have had a great experience and would encourage any woman to pursue a career in FinTech, but there is a massive lack of diverse representation at senior and board level and that has a real knock on effect'. When women are undervalued, they don't get recognised for their work and they certainly don't get promoted, irrelevant of their capability or success. For us to be working in an industry with such forward-thinking attributes it should be surprising to all that we have been unable to make enough actionable steps to effectively impact this subject.

Thankfully, a number of women have been able to break through these barriers, albeit not enough—and from all that I have learnt—they have certainly not been engaged on a 'level playing field'. This term 'level playing field' has been used by many of the women and men in my various podcast series to describe how certain groups in the workplace don't receive the same experience, often being held back due to their circumstance or working alongside others who find it easier to progress. Angela Yore is the Managing Director and Founder of a Public Relations firm specifically for FinTechs. She is incredibly active in driving inclusion across the industry, being on the advisory board of the EWPN, the Inclusion Foundation and another woman featured on the Innovate Finance Powerlist, this time as part of the coveted 'Standout 35' for 2020. She was very clear about workplaces needing to change to deliver a 'level playing field' stating, 'some people are better at pushing themselves forward, which doesn't necessarily mean they are better. Workplaces have a responsibility to provide opportunities to everybody'. Calling herself an activist, Angela drives change and demands that we challenge one another. Like me, she believes in leaving a legacy and part of that legacy is very much in everybody being given a fair chance for accessing opportunities with their employers whether they have the personality to ask for it or not.

When this doesn't happen, we often see main caregivers side-lined in the workplace, not for working less hours, but for working less visible or non-standard hours. The blame for the inequity is put on societal perceptions of women, legal miscarriages of justice, the fact that women do most of the care for both younger and older generations, and so forth. This all adds to the way women are then perceived at work. When women have needed flexibility in time, location, and presenteeism, historically this has been seen to mean they are 'less committed'. When women have had to leave a meeting to attend a sick child or parent it has meant they have missed out on the final decision-making. Or more importantly that group has missed out on their input on any final decision-making. We haven't historically lived in a world where these meetings have taken place in 'family' friendly hours as the majority don't have this lived experience; and as Caroline Hughes said, they haven't been 'curious' outside their own experience. These commonplace behaviours have contributed to the generic and unconscious bias we all have towards women in the workplace.

Akita Somani, the Chief of Staff and Diversity and Inclusion Champion at Elavon Europe believes that we all carry bias in our everyday lives and moreover when we are interacting with people from diverse backgrounds at work. As a business that strives to empower payment options for customers of all shapes and sizes, she drives progress on this subject by calling out that any sort of bias in the workplace 'prevents us from operating at an optimum capacity'. Unconscious Bias has been a topic discussed in the workplace for a number of years now, and has been the topic of many training sessions because it is a clear barrier to progress and robust outcomes. The ideal state would be to make all of us more self-aware and call out Unconscious Bias when we see it, especially with the assumption that most of us may have the best intentions, and yet not quite cognisant of how seemingly insignificant remarks or behaviours could set others back and deprive us of the opportunity to truly benefit from the diverse perspectives around us.

The Chief Operating Officer of Cashflows, Helen Smith, agreed but called for more action than just the odd training session. She said back in early 2019 that when thinking about 'how we can create and build effective organisations, the key is self-awareness and emotional intelligence and that is something that organisations and leaders can develop in their people. This is central to changing our own individual unconscious bias'. For her it is actually about getting to the root of the problem and realising 'how comfortable or not people are with differences' and then addressing that properly. If we have this barrier up because of who we perceive a person to be, we simply miss out on wonderful experiences to make us all better. I felt enlightened by the simplicity of the suggestion when Helena Nordegren, a Sales executive of Finastra said in her podcast, 'if you feel comfortable and safe in yourself, you will include people. Those who are afraid or insecure need a group of like-minded people surrounding them, people who agree with only them and exclude others'. Helena has worked in a number of Banks before joining Finastra and shared her views on tackling individual and cultural leadership mindsets to affect positive change. This change is about challenging the traditions and status quo to pave the way for stronger teams and businesses. Going back to what Akita said, 'It's not enough to not discriminate. It's also important to move towards the other end of the spectrum of being an ally, and to make that journey you need to have self-awareness and recognition of your behaviour'. This recognition is an everyday task where I believe, day in, and day out, we all have a responsibility to make note and raise our hands to the bias we see and the inequality that takes place. Without this too many situations pass us by and work to bolster the system we are trying to dissolve.

Sometimes the system allows for women not just to be excluded and overlooked but just as damaging, to be side-lined too. Sarah Carver, Global Head of Digital at a global managed services, technology solutions and consulting provider called Delta Capita was very open about the environment she had witnessed for women earlier in her career and particularly whilst having children. Sarah focuses on digital, customer-led propositions, change management, and strategy and has worked across the breadth of Financial Services including financial exchanges, capital markets, retail and commercial banking, and wealth management which gives us huge amounts of insight when she said the following;

'Take the lead role, don't settle for being the person who does all the work backstage but not being the actor that gets on stage at the end. I've watched it with a lot of women who can often be the brains behind the operation, the strategists but they get sidelined'. I have seen this too many times, where the detail, the process, the execution of tasks is credited to the 'actor' that gets on stage at the end without even a small nod or citation to the woman who put in all the work and effort. Ultimately, it's such short-term thinking and incredibly non-strategic but it will only change when the leadership is prepared to call out this behaviour and focus on actually instilling a level playing field. There are many examples of endless diversity and inclusion policies and corporate statements which are on a wall somewhere but not truly baked into the company's core values. Sarah does believe however that employees are helping to drive the change with the increased focus on ESG in the industry and companies' actions. Tick box activities no longer cut it, talent will move en-masse where employees observe themselves or others being treated unequally making DEI not just the right thing to do but also the right business decision.

A number of women shared their experiences around how they have managed to have their voice heard throughout their career. Many have had pivotal roles in businesses but still recalled spending years in board rooms being not only the sole woman but also some stated how they were the only woman from an ethnic minority background. One person in particular said that she had to learn quickly and that 'many times I had to be very loud to get heard but I have a lot of self-belief'. Let us imagine the experience for someone without that self-belief? Perhaps they wouldn't be heard, perhaps they would learn not to speak up, perhaps they wouldn't have got there at all. Another person shared more: she was told that she was 'aggressive', she was told to 'tone it down' yet her message to all of us, male or female, is 'take feedback but never stop letting your voice get heard'. Her experience was about being a minority in the room and having to overcompensate to be heard on the same par as her white male counterparts.

In talks with Joanne Dewar, the Chief Executive Officer of Global Processing Services, she highlighted her experience of leading her boardroom conversations; 'I need to speak in not my natural voice' and 'I have to hit really hard to be heard'. As Chief Executive Officer she has invested into her board members and wider team to 'level the playing field', and ensure that women following her don't need to work harder than their counterparts to get their point across. An example of this is when she said, 'I educate our board on how they need to hear other people so they can hear others with different character sets'. Looking at these different character sets it is when I hear a communication void the most often. This void enables and perpetuates inequity. Anna Flach spoke of it saying, 'men communicate differently and there are subconscious biases. When I first joined the technology sector, it was hard for me to get that credibility'. Taking this further, many women cited examples of where they hadn't yet spoken in a meeting, but their mere existence was presumed less senior by their male counterparts. Whilst not all women have this experience, I have been offered evidence upon evidence in support of understanding that it is not an occasional incident.

Alexandra Boyle, yet another award-winning woman in FinTech has said 'I have walked into the room, and it's been assumed that I am less than knowledgeable and that they would prefer to speak to a male colleague. You don't really forget those moments'. Alexandra has a Bachelor's degree in Finance, she has worked for a global private equity group, the New York Stock Exchange, and was one of the first members to join the team at OpenFin in 2014. OpenFin is an incredibly successful FinTech providing operating systems to over 1500 financial firms worldwide. They stand for innovation and agility, and she is now their Head of Strategic Client Group for Europe. Being in the position has meant that she has had to approach the assumed credibility issue in a 'collaborative way by having a constructive approach'. In essence she said, 'I address exactly who I am early on'.

A similar response to this type of situation was cited by Katharine Wooller. Katharine spoke to me as Managing Director of Dacxi, one of the most successful players in Cryptocurrency today. She has built numerous FinTechs from conception to having turnovers of hundreds of millions of pounds. She said, 'I wish I had a pound for every time I went to a meeting, and someone expected me to write notes. No, I would say, actually I'm Global Head of Clients'. The sheer credibility and power of these women make these encounters even more astonishing, but they happen time and time again. What varies hugely is how they were dealt with and the effect on each individual it has happened to. Every woman in the industry will be able to recollect a similar experience. Leda Gylptis, Chief Client Officer of 10x Banking, a business that provides a cloud native banking platform, spoke of her early career and how she didn't need to 'fight those battles'. Remembering her time working for the Bank of New York Mellon she praised her line manager, his boss and her boss above her too saying; 'did I have to deal with sexism? Did I have to deal with inappropriate remarks? Sure! Did I have people talking over me and dismissing me? Of course! But I also had allies who actually went to battle for me when that happened'. Leda's message wasn't to highlight the discrimination but instead celebrate her mentors and supporters as she felt they had facilitated a foundation on which she could stand up for herself in her career.

For each of these women, these negative moments were never the ones they lingered on when sharing their career journey with me. Instead, they were a brief recollection and our conversation focused on their successes, despite working within a system where this happened again and again.

I have only highlighted three of the many examples I have heard. When I think back to how women have communicated, from Joanne Dewar, not in her 'natural voice' to others being told to 'tone it down' I am reminded of the excellent points Felicitas Coulibaly raised in her podcast. She very clearly pointed out 'when women speak their mind, it triggers people'. She highlighted how people react to their managers and noted that it was hugely different depending on the gender of that manager. For these women they are left in an impossible position. When they 'are firm, they are called bossy or bitchy', then on the other hand they are often 'accused of being too sensitive' and in directing their team they often face 'disrespectful communication' including those not taking them seriously or 'laughing off' clear instructions. Felictas is the Global Head of Inside Sales at Mambu and now that she herself is building a team around her, she is more passionate than ever to give the right people with potential the chances they need. Mambu is a cloud banking platform that empowers their customers to build and change banking products easily. Their mission is very much linked to her personal drive for taking a more enlightened approach to building stronger teams through empowerment. She recollects much earlier days in her career where, as a woman, 'your every move is questioned, and you have to fight harder to be taken seriously' and strives to break this cycle for those coming through the talent pipeline behind her.

This notion that 'firm' women are received very differently to 'firm' men was also mentioned by Leda, who said 'when you see a woman leading with a forceful approach you are being told to 'Calm down dear'... I'm very calm you are just wrong'. We hear it, and we see it time and time again. Apart from Leda's time at BNY Mellon most of the cases I hear about, the woman in question was left to defend her title, role, or stature without an ally. It is often in this defence that she is then undermined. We are seeing similar encounters for other minorities in the workplace.

Nilixa Devlukia, the Founder of Payments Solved and a payments, digital currency, crypto assets, and open banking expert, spoke of her experience and referred to microaggressions. 'As women' she stated, 'we are often challenged in being heard, in being taken seriously and I've come to notice over time that there are lots of little ways you can be undermined'. She felt it was these microaggressions that in their multiples are detrimental. She recalled being spoken over, being ignored, feeling undervalued, taken for granted, and actively overlooked in meeting with her colleagues. She said this wasn't just a face-to-face occurrence but could even happen over email too. She was clear to outline that the call to action has to be about plucking up the courage to report such behaviour. 'It's a brave step as it's very easy to be seen as the troublemaker or the moaner', everyone who feels undermined she argued, needs to trust their instinct and act upon it.

What Nilixa described next is all too familiar to all of us, either as perpetrators or victims of this. Any attempt at highlighting the problem is often met with rebuttals. 'It's easy to justify bad behaviour' she continued, as excuses are often found, or you are told the incident wasn't as bad as you recall. Often you are told it wasn't intended and that you have been the dreaded, 'over sensitive'. Whilst small slights and inconsistencies happen through forgetfulness or the normal run of events, when they create a consistent pattern of behaviour over a prolonged period, there should be no doubt that the case for over sensitivity is utterly void. Unfortunately, this casual dismissal of behavioural sleights is all too commonplace, where those who have a duty of care to their staff, perpetuate the system by their failure to act. Instead, we see rebuttals, and this is why I started this chapter highlighting the Heijer quote; because we have to change the system should we ever wish to achieve a flower in bloom in our environments. Systemic change has to start with our ability to recognise every day and 'normalised' negative behaviours or interactions. We must start with ourselves and address our own bias of expectation and assumption.

Kelly Read-Parish raised the issue that new women joining financial firms often feel they have to change their mannerisms and interests in order to fit in in a traditionally male-dominated environment. Kelly is the Chief Operating Officer of Credit Kudos, a FinTech building intelligent tools for lenders using open banking data to enable better credit decisions. From her over a decade long experience within both technology-driven and more traditional financial firms, she lays blame at a broader cultural system where men often fear being seen as feminine, and women are encouraged to adopt cultural markers of masculinity in order to be taken seriously as professionals. 'A realignment needs to happen in society as well as in the workplace to make women feel they don't have to act more male in order to be successful'. Kelly would like to see firms foster an environment where a variety of perspectives are respected as both professional and valid. She cites the frequent low-level disparagement of traditionally feminine interests—from fashion to child rearing—especially in financial workplaces as just one example of the subtle pressures on women to adapt to traditionally male environments in order to improve perception of their capabilities. 'There is no quick-fix solution', she continues, 'but the more individuals share their diverse perspectives, especially women in more powerful positions, the more acceptable mirroring those behaviours becomes at every level'.

Emmanuelle Mathey gave similar advice when we recorded her podcast. She spoke about how psychological safety in the workplace is cultivated. Emmanuelle is another woman from a non-STEM background having studied law and moved into the financial services sector following that. Now she is Group Head of Credit and Co-Chief Risk Officer for Wealth Management at Schroders, an Investment Management firm. She said it's simply about laying out the expectations and following up on them with consistent action, 'create a safe place where people are encouraged to contribute and challenge'. She tells people again and again 'it's your job to disagree with me, that's why you are here'. For Emmanuelle the safety we talk about is simply about making sure people feel their opinions are valued and that they trust in the environment that they can comment, question, and debate freely. So passionate about this point she added 'it is about letting them be different' because if 'no one is willing to speak up we have missed an opportunity'. The reality of this is not easy she jovially admitted but so worth the reward. For every new idea and business suggestion, sometimes she smiled, 'you just want them to agree'. This is often a point of failure where we see many managers, senior, middle, or 'accidental', who simply aren't ready to be questioned, who feel it is an attack on their authority and are simply not trained in what good management should entail. These 'accidental' managers, as Emmanuelle phrases it, are those who have been put into managerial positions because they were good at the execution of their role, but without appropriate training and support around people management.

Whilst true psychological safety in the workplace still seems a long way off. Kate Bohn, a multiple award-winning Innovation and Strategy Lead, mentor to the financial services community, networker and connector in the space, is considered an expert. She is a passionate advocate for building this psychological safety and was quick to remind me that in many environments the team is still ruled by managers who find their own safety only in others agreeing with them. Kate is the epitome of creative and lateral thinking, unique opinions, and asking, 'what can we do differently to make this better?' Kate prides this diversity of perspective on her background. Yet again we have another woman who didn't study STEM, instead she followed a path that took her to Art, Art

History, Marketing and eCommerce across a bachelor's and master's degree. With this experience she believes the industry can thrive on dynamism and humanism in the workplace. She says people will be truly 'creative if you let them'. Furthermore, she talks about STEAM rather than STEM and that STEM becomes stronger when Arts is considered. To explain this, she says the humanity aspect cannot be overlooked as only with this considered can 'we understand the real pinch point' that needs to be solved and the purpose of the solution we are providing. The 'why' lies within the person, the 'how' lies within technology. 'We are human beings, not human doings, and we have robots and automation for the "doings"'.

This type of thinking has not been the norm and hasn't necessarily been accepted easily. Being the minority who thinks, feels, and communicates this way can be a very lonely place. This is particularly prevalent for people voicing their alternate line of thought and I hear example upon example (of women in particular) receiving rebuttals, condescension and nothing other than fob offs when trying to have these different perspectives heard. Over the years we have come a long way away from the general acceptance of aggressive and open discrimination however there have been far too many examples I have heard about which fit under the headline of 'passive discrimination'.

I constantly see this in board rooms or meetings involving external parties where the environment is high conflict, ultra-competitive, and aggressive. Often ideas are argued against because they can be—not because it is right—and winning becomes more important than listening or collaborating. Passive discrimination is often cited in the continued use of unconscious or rather conscious bias. A number of businesses have invested in training sessions to educate the unconscious bias in their teams, but I never really hear about the follow-up or the ramifications to the perpetrators of sustained bias. Rather than investigating or addressing the bias, I often hear the person who raised concerns or the person on the receiving end of it have been forcefully placated or given some arbitrary rationalisation as to why it wasn't as bad as they felt it was. They are encouraged to not 'rock the boat' and in danger of being tagged as 'difficult'.

When discussing my concerns over the vast array of women who had shared these experiences confidentially, Kate described it as 'death by 1000 paper cuts'. Too many women are facing issues in the workplace that don't just make it harder to thrive, but harder to survive and more difficult to drive their careers forward. It can be a struggle to be heard, seen, acknowledged, and valued, and she is at pains to point out that there is a distinct difference between 'hard' and 'harmful'. When consistently repeated over time, these experiences don't make it easy for women in the workplace and Kate intimated this slow demise and attrition from seemingly 'little' things can be a significant player in breaking a person's resilience and mental health. When the evidence doesn't support the brush-off response to reporting these behaviours, the person on the receiving end should be entitled to expect some duty of care from their management. For me, it's what's often described or shrugged off as a 'misunderstanding' yet can be incredibly detrimental to our entire community and its future success. The ramifications of not dealing with the '1000 paper cuts' appropriately holds us back as an industry and stands firmly in the way of us embracing true diversity of thought.

We mustn't forget the simplicity of being the minority voice and presence in the workplace and how that is perceived and accepted by the majority. Alexandra Boyle had raised this exact point, 'It's not unusual for me to be the only women in a meeting and I wish it was unusual' and because of this we still have a system weighted towards the majority. So far, I have highlighted the 'system' as the workplace itself, I am a recruiter in my nature and the 'system' of how people enter the workplace also needs to be explored. Looking at the different drivers in people when applying for jobs, I have had years of experience. I also reached out to a number of the UK leading online job boards to back up my own research surrounding this. When considering the main factors that drive technologists to new job opportunities it is interesting to break this down across those who identified as male or female. Drawing upon thousands of job applications and the data derived from those applications it becomes quickly apparent that men were drawn to jobs with competitive base salaries, new technology and innovation, whereas the majority of women who applied were largely driven by a flexible working environment, a work–life balance, leaders who supported them and a friendly working environment.

I found this data exactly in line with the thousands of applicants Harrington Starr support. Everyone is different and motivated by different things but looking at the statistics each of the job boards produced online I wasn't surprised. For years we have seen evidence that women are less likely to apply to overly demanding jobs adverts and are massively turned off by endless lists of skills. We know that the majority of women won't apply to these adverts if they possess eight out of ten of the skills listed, believing they are not qualified. Men on the other hand will apply with far less. A societal issue perhaps but one that we can tackle by changing the way we recruit, changing our adverts and changing how we attract new talent to companies. Samantha Knights the Head of IT Architecture at Ninety One, explains it so clearly when she said, 'if you look at job specifications and how they are written in the technology industry, "Rockstar" of this, "pushing the boundaries" of that and a lot of aggressive language. It can often put people off applying'. She went on to admit this aggressive language had stopped her from applying for several roles in her lifetime even though she would describe herself as a technologist that constantly pushes the boundaries. At NinetyOne Asset Management Samantha has the responsibility of ensuring the technology architecture is sound and continuously moves in the direction of target by overseeing and coaching. She is architectural head of the entire technology suite that enables the investors to make a real difference to their clients, helping them to achieve their long-term goals. Even with this under her belt, 'Rockstar' isn't a term she is drawn to. When we focus on this for a second it seems almost impossible that businesses haven't made more progress so far and that we still hear this type of language used freely and often in blissful ignorance.

When considering job interviews themselves, it can be very off-putting if women don't have visibility of other females in the company when interviewed. Gabriel MacSweeney, Strategic Partnerships and Commercial Strategy at Codat spoke highly of her Codat interview experience. Founded in 2017, Codat is a forward-thinking FinTech that powers the connectivity to financial products and services used by small businesses. Values wise, the business is about being useful, united, and unstoppable and this is reflected in their challenging yet welcoming interview process, as Gabriel described. However, she was quick to highlight that this hasn't always been her experience. 'In the past, I've found it very noticeable and off-putting when there's a lack of females involved in the interview process'. This is a shame, firstly for businesses who haven't been able to include a female in the process because they don't have any and a shame for those businesses that didn't think for a moment that a person interviewing may like to see someone they can relate to.

Having worked hard to raise awareness and ignite change actions across the industry since 2015 these figures have driven me to strive for so much more action. I have many solutions to this which I will outline in the following chapters, solutions which are yielding some fantastic results and driving real change.

The reality is that the perception of FinTech and financial services as unwelcoming, un-family friendly, long hours, overly competitive cultures is still in existence. We only need to read the big news headlines of 2020 and 2021 where the CHIEF EXECUTIVE OFFICER of Goldman Sachs called working from home during the pandemic an 'aberration' and in later news headlines his suggestions of a return to a '95 hour working week in the office' to see why so many people are turned off. What we will see however is that there are a lot of unsung stories and heroic firms who are truly walking the talk by taking real change actions to be more inclusive and build environments for everyone, not just the few. Personally, I feel excluded by this type of conversation. Having regularly worked 15-hour days in my career, I was a believer that the harder I worked the more recognition I would get, the more committed I would seem and the further I would progress. I thought this was the only way to do myself and my career justice until I learnt there were other ways. I gave birth to my daughter in early 2020 and I had to learn very quickly that I didn't have the luxury of my 15-hour days anymore. I had to get my work done faster, be more productive, I had to be more efficient, and I absolutely love how effective I have become and thank her for that every day. Thinking back to the many conversations I have had around new mothers returning to the workplace we can identify another point of failure for women, maternity.

Many have called it out saying 'it's not a holiday' and beseeching that we must 'stop calling it that'. These derogatory comments are still commonplace and whether in jest or not do very little for how women returning to work feel valued. This is seen in the statistics, not specific to FinTech but for the UK workforce as a whole—we see 29% of first-time mums not returning to work. Peoplemanagement.co.uk surveyed 1000 mothers in the workplace and found that only 18% felt happy and confident about returning to work, whilst 37% felt so unhappy and isolated upon their return that they seriously considered leaving. It is often the vernacular that we are losing mothers from the workforce because they want to stay at home and raise their children full time. Looking at these statistics, coupled with the thousands of conversations I have had with new mothers returning to work over my career, we can no longer brush this loss off as a 'mother's choice'. There will be a percentage of women who will choose to become full-time mothers and the sheer cost of childcare cannot be overlooked either. However, this isn't the only reason. The point I wish to raise is that there is that currently not enough being done to support mothers on their return to work, and that many have told me they felt they couldn't come back, and if they did, they found it very difficult. Ionna Stanegloudi, who we met earlier, said it was this that drove her to found Finclude. 'It's been so liberating' she exclaimed, 'I was fed up by so many things in the corporate world, I work from wherever and whenever. What is invaluable for me is the flexibility and freedom'. So many agree with her and I repeatedly hear how archaic expectations of staff and legacy cultures of 'presenteeism' are driving some away and acting as a barrier to attracting new talent to the field.

I have raised these issues to define the 'system' we blame for many of the barriers to gender equality in the workplace. I feel we will continue to struggle to change if we don't acknowledge how this 'system' hinders progression. When we looked at the multitude of gaps—from the pay gap, to the board gap, to the promotion gap, to the funding gap, I wanted to reflect on how the workplace environment can facilitate the continuity of such gaps. Moreover, a huge topic for further discussion will be around this not being an issue for the minority, but instead a call to action for everyone in the workplace to solve. Emmy Granström, the Marketing Director of SteelEye, a financial compliance and data analytics provider, felt passionately about this point. When discussing how we change the gender imbalance in FinTech she questioned, 'why should the onus be on women and not the system? We need to stop telling women to change'. Emmy, like many other women in the industry, frequently finds that she is expected to take on the responsibility for debunking any misconceptions on behalf of her male counterparts. Women regularly find themselves quizzed over whether there really is a problem and being the only person willing to highlight endemic pinch points and what needs to change in the system.

In talks with Alex Ford, the VP of Product and Marketing for Encompass Corporation, said similar, 'fix the system not the woman, the system is stacked against her'. Alex has worked at Encompass since its early days and has contributed to the growth of this unique data-driven FinTech. They automate gathering, processing, and collation of information. Coming from a coaching and leadership background, Alex identifies that all too often, members of the workplace dismiss the gender struggle by saying the woman involved needs to behave differently or brush up certain skills in order to be seen or heard. 'Putting that responsibility on the individual alone to overcome years and years of bias and systemic disadvantage is completely unrealistic and unfair' she explained.

I am well aware these shortcomings are not unique to finance or technology or FinTech, which is why I wanted to raise them so clearly here. The purpose of deconstructing exactly what is meant by changing the 'system', starts with the acknowledgement of the many harmful workplace behaviours and cultures showcased in this chapter. We have to work together to accept that these exist, accept that they have an inappropriate and detrimental effect on people, and then agree that we will be part of the change. The solutions we are uncovering and delivering in FinTech will work everywhere, for everyone, and together this problem can be solved.

7

Movement: Sharing the Steps Forward

With everything that we have looked at so far it is important to celebrate those who are making real change across the industry and defining new norms in doing so. The problem of the gender imbalance and its impact has been identified and acknowledged by many of the players across the Financial Services and FinTech community. This is driving action we haven't ever seen before. With the rise of mission led businesses and the need for agility, innovation and diversity of thought this topic is increasingly prevalent on the agenda of any business determined to succeed. I want to outline the good work I have seen.

Kenzy Goodwin, an experienced senior leader within the industry, said we are 'seeing a whole new level of effort' to address the gender imbalance. Kenzy has worked in the financial services for well over 20 years now, having worked for the global investment manager, Blackrock as a Senior Equity Trader for two decades and now as Partner of Finceler8, a company dedicated to accelerating FinTech engagement with financial markets. Kenzy has been able to see the industry through a variety of lenses and believes what we can identify as change now is quite different from what we have seen in previous attempts. We must celebrate the good steps we have been making to be able to expand on them.

Since the mid-2010s we have seen a meteoric rise in networking events, panel discussions, and award ceremonies to debate hot topics, to educate, to share knowledge, and to celebrate the individuals across the space. These

© The Author(s), under exclusive license to Springer Nature
Switzerland AG 2022
N. Edwards-Dashti, *FinTech Women Walk the Talk*,
https://doi.org/10.1007/978-3-030-90574-3_7

networking events would often have a speaker scheduled to share information about a new regulation, an exciting new technology or perhaps to share insights from their sector or specialism. The people who attend would have time to mingle before and after the talk to learn from one another as well as the speaker of the session. Panel events have been similar, they allowed for several people to debate a topic and share ideas, often raising awareness of a problem and discussing how it can be solved. We have seen lots of diversity and inclusion debates such as these to draw upon numerous experiences and give a voice to a number of people. Rahma Javed, the Director of Engineering at Deliveroo, raised the point that the 'first step towards solving any problem is the awareness aspect of it, the acceptance or realisation of it'. The communities that are fostered around these events and the organisations that build these networking groups regularly hold awards with application processes and judging panels. A great example of this is one which I have mentioned numerous times already, and that is 'The Women in FinTech Powerlist', a yearly award run by the independent not-for-profit body Innovate Finance. Every year they receive thousands of applications and nominations from across the industry for women who have contributed to the space. Their judging panels award the top 150 women they deem to have contributed to the industry above and beyond their working role the coveted title of being on the 'Powerlist'. Innovate Finance are not the only ones who host their own awards. We see WearetheCity, FinTech Futures and their Banking in Tech awards, FinTech Magazine, WomeninTech and many more. 100Women in FinTech, of which Kenzy Goodwin is the Vice Chair, is a global visibility initiative recognising senior female FinTech professionals that are making an impact in the sector and actively elevates their public profiles, enabling their stronger interconnectivity to the FinTech ecosystem and inspiring the next generation of female FinTech talent. The network is regularly called upon by the media, conference organisers and industry practitioners for female FinTech experts to contribute to industry panels. Organisations partner with businesses to support them through education, training and consulting to offer solutions to the diversity problem we face. There has been a steady increase of groups growing within business to raise awareness and provide support to people working there. Many of the people I celebrate in this book run their own internal network group for their company to discuss challenges parents, LGBTQ+, ethnic minority, neurodiverse and women face, and tackle these together in safe spaces, events, or discussions. Supporting one another and building comradery to ignite confidence and well-being for their teams.

When the team at Wirex decided to launch their own awards, they focused on their sector and named it the 'Rising Women in Crypto Power

List'. Wirex is a crypto-friendly payments platform that is working hard to make crypto and traditional currencies equal and accessible to all through a number of products and campaigns. The introduction of their multi-currency payments card has allowed for so much recognition and normalisation of cryptocurrencies to the average spender.

Their launch of the 'Rising Women in Crypto Power List' in 2020 had the same mission; to raise the awareness of the crypto space but also to showcase the amazing women making waves in the space. I supported their launch with one of my podcasts and had the pleasure of speaking with Jenny Kong, Global Head of Marketing, who described their purpose as 'we want to show other women that this is an amazing and hugely growing industry'.

The perception of new digital currencies such as Bitcoin is often that of risk, scepticism, and uncertainty. Jenny and the team have been working hard to debunk these perceptions alongside highlighting the lucrative and exciting career prospects this space has for women. She continued 'we love our jobs, other women and next generation must know it's an option and a good one!'

I completely agree with this method of bringing confidence to the industry through evidence and case studies. The importance of having visible women in leadership shouldn't be underestimated. For many, role models are the people they see, and we are seeing many more women in leadership positions than ever before. I have made a concerted effort for the past few years to celebrate the feats of the women in this industry through my video series, magazines, podcast series, whitepapers, and presentations. If we all showcase our successes, women working within this industry will become the norm. In addition, the confidence is also growing within the women who are celebrated. The platforms given by the events raise the credibility and awareness of the women themselves as well as the topics they discuss. The awards shine a light on the individuals who are driving change and are standout in their sector, again giving positive reinforcement to a minority in the space. The value of this is huge on a personal as well as wider level.

It was something that Alexandra Boyle, Head of Strategic Client Group Europe of OpenFin felt strongly about too. 'It's important to elevate and amplify women's careers in FinTech panels and events, this allows for more representation across the board, building a proactive community of women and allies as well as a spotlight for the voices and careers of women'. The people involved and in turn their companies are normalising the gender balance discussion and as a consequence are giving themselves more opportunity to change it. We all need to accept that a balanced workforce won't just happen, we will have to work on it. Celebrating the careers, successes, and challenges overcome by the women in this space is a powerful way of doing this. If more people are seeing the need to increase diversity everywhere they look, more people will get excited about it and commit to taking action themselves.

I passionately believe in relatable role models. Having worked in the financial technology recruitment sector since leaving university I am also within a heavily male-dominated world. There may have been the odd female role model but certainly none that I felt I could relate to or anyone I aspired to be. This wasn't a reflection of the few women in my space, instead a lack of access to them. This has been a huge driver for me in the way I recorded my podcast series—never too scripted or prepared but instead great conversations with people about their story, their journey, and their lessons along the way. I loved it when Lauren McEwan, the Records Manager, at the Pension Protection Fund said, 'I respond really well to representation, seeing someone you identify with doing something cool or something you haven't thought of before plants a seed in your mind'. Lauren never thought she could become so interested in data, and in her podcast laughed to think how the management and security of data has become such a passion. She attributes much of her success in the field to the support of bosses past and present, and is grateful to the senior women leaders who influenced her early career by achieving and paving the way.

In talks with Roisin Levine, the Head of Banks at Flux, a digital receipt data company, she felt that visibility would have a positive effect on next-generation talent. Saying, 'its common sense to have more women in prominent roles and role models will be very important to attract more to the industry', she argued the point that positive reinforcement would become its own self-fulfilling prophecy.

This raises the topic of what I like to call 'next generation inspiration', where people and their companies within the FinTech community are investing their time into educating school children, speaking at universities to share career journeys and sharing success stories with people outside of the marketplace to attract them to it. Eimear O'Connor, The Chief Operating Officer of Form3 believes, 'society and the world of work has certainly come a long way, it's great to see so many exciting movements to encourage girls to study STEM subjects and women to start careers in very traditionally male dominated world'. Form3 is a payment technology company and employs the full spectrum of technology staff to design, build, and run the technology that powers the future of payments. Eimear recognises the challenges of building gender diversity in male-dominated industries but is keen to focus on solutions for today as well as tomorrow—instead of just accepting that the senior engineering pool is today predominately male, her recruitment team has a specific focus on attracting and retaining senior and experienced female engineering talent too. Eimear also believes that creating even a small pool of female engineers now will have a significant impact on the company's ability to attract female engineering talent in the future. Eimear recognises that there is a long way to go but in the immediate term, strategies such as 'over emphasising' targets on female talent ensures this remains a management team objective. She links this directly to the fact that 'we must recognise that as a society both inside and outside of the workplace there are still huge inequalities that exist whether it's in education, political engagement, access to family leave, health or income and these gaps are still too big'. This is a driver for Eimear and the team who are extremely active in their work to increase diversity in the workplace. They do so by partnering with the organisations I mentioned as well as being agile enough to try new ways of identifying new staff. This is an area I will explore more deeply in later chapters.

Visa are also big believers in giving back, Tribeni Chougule, their Head of Change Management, told me how they have 'focussed on attracting, retaining and developing our female talent by engaging with schools and graduates to ensure they know the opportunities for working with Visa and that technology is a world you can be part of'. Having spoken to students at a number of university events myself, I know that the recurring issue is that younger generations don't know enough about the career prospects within FinTech nor do they believe it is a welcoming place for them. Companies are now seeing that this is their responsibility to change these perceptions and encourage 'next generation inspiration'. It is amazing to see so much work going into future talent pipelining. Companies that partner with or set up their own groups are finding it easier to stand out as a company of choice. Some examples of groups that businesses are partnering with to invest in future talent include, Codegirlsfirst, Little Miss Geek, Digigirls, Stemettes, Geek Girls, and Get with the Program.

The work I do partnering with universities is so rewarding. Dispelling the myths around the FinTech community and instilling confidence that we are an industry that wants to invest in new people and new ways of thinking is a hard task but one I believe we will make headway in if we all play our part.

Looking at school level there have been some interesting debates around what happens to young girls and their interest in the sciences. For example, in a roundtable I hosted, Celine Crawford, the Chief Communications Officer of Smarkets remarked, 'when you look at girls and boys at 9 years old there's absolutely no difference in their cognitive abilities, girls are taught they are not good at maths or they are made to feel they are not good at maths and you see then drop out'. The awareness of this and discussion within FinTech businesses is a huge step forward however much more can and should be done about this phenomenon. In line with my thoughts on blaming the flower for not blooming, I don't buy the cop out that girls don't like maths, technology, or science. Nor does Jeni Trice, the Founder of Get with the Program, a business dedicated to educating school children in a fun and engaging way. Her mission is to 'reach kids who may not naturally choose computing, those who don't think it's for them or haven't got the tools available'. She wants to help children learn about the wonder of technology, capture their imaginations, and most importantly dispel this myth that technology is only for a small demographic. She asks businesses to sponsor her work to allow her to scale up and make gains within the educational system, and we are seeing more and more firms use CSR initiatives to help get the next generation thinking about STEM careers.

Finastra is another business leading the way in this. Chirine BenZaied-Bourgerie, Head of Innovation, was clear when she commented, 'female empowerment starts with girl empowerment'. She discussed how we could help erase gender gaps and felt that 'we need to consider girls as well as boys and how we educate them'. Finastra is busy with the active inclusion work it does both internally and externally and it has a fantastic group of people who drive different campaigns and initiatives. The team runs hackathons, regular events, and panel discussions to keep inclusion topics high on the agenda and actionable follow-up projects always ensue to encourage gender balance. I have had the privilege of judging a number of the hackathons and have found it such an eye-opening experience that I encourage as many businesses as possible follow suit. An example of the type of hackathon Finastra runs is called 'Hack to the Future: Build an unbiased FinTech Future', where hundreds of submissions are received from around the world from teams of people with ideas for businesses, products and systems to eradicate bias. It is incredibly empowering and heightens industry as well as individual recognition. It is so awe-inspiring to see such talent and unique perspectives coming from students, FinTech enthusiasts, and also people outside the industry that it makes you realise how much untapped talent is out there for us to attract to this changing industry.

Rashmi Prabhakar, the Chief of Staff at Finastra, said that when she was talking at a university mentoring programme, a female student posed a question to her asking, 'Is FinTech a tough environment for me "as a female" to have a successful career?' Rashmi's response highlighted the need to have a strong belief in herself, take risks, follow our dreams, and focused on leveraging our education and skills irrespective of our gender, thus helping the student see all the opportunities that lay ahead of her and achieving her goals and dreams without creating hurdles or obstacles in her own mind. This is another stark example of the work needed to change perceptions of the workplace and a further call to action that we are behave in a way where these perceptions aren't true.

The reality is that the industry needs to ensure negative perceptions are incorrect through action. This needs to be twofold, firstly the businesses and their staff must go out to the industry to actively myth bust through events, talks, advertising, representation, empowerment of current staff, and all the awareness I have been discussing. Secondly, FinTech and financial services institutions must work to hire potential and invest in them and their training. Moreover, this potential should come from people from all sorts of backgrounds and experiences to truly allow these businesses to 'walk the talk' for diversity of thought. As one of the original members of the HUBX team, Maya Aweida had been really clear on this stating that at graduate level the gender balance 'should be fifty-fifty, as its about raw talent and they can grow the business as you train them into more specific roles'. She has been a big believer in trying different things out in her career and felt that people will be allowed to grow into different types of roles if only they are given the chance to learn and be invested in.

Celine gives us another example of how actionable change can be driven, this time through internal networking. She created a Diversity and Inclusion committee in her business to 'engage people across team, levels, experience and locations to bring to the fore issues that are important to them'. This had led robust change in their hiring processes. Examples ranged from women being part of interview panels, to correct language in job adverts and training interviewers on how to conduct unbiased interviews and inclusive interviews.

This is absolutely key for Kelly Read-Parish, the Chief Operating Officer for Credit Kudos. She is a big advocate for simply getting this right by demanding change in how we recruit, 'we need to have a more inclusive viewpoint of not writing job descriptions that just appeal to things that stereotypically apply to men'. She went on to share her experience of how women tend to favour job descriptions that have a more collaborative approach that talks about working with a team, saying that all of us if we wish to incite change must make steps 'to understand your audience and whether they feel a job advert is made for them'. We are seeing this more and more, with many businesses ensuring that their adverts for new members of staff were genderless and that their employment contracts don't only refer to the new employees as 'he'.

We have seen an exponential rise in the role of Diversity and Inclusion Champions or Leads within the sector. This has immediately increased visibility of the subject and daily mindfulness from members of the team who wouldn't consider diversity or inclusion their issue. There have been many hugely successful people who I celebrate in these pages who have this title and lots of responsibility to make changes across their business. Many drive the good steps I celebrate but they need support from everyone else in the business. For all the successes I celebrate, it's crucial to mention that without sponsorship and support from business executives a lot of these things become futile quickly. The internal groups that have built the most momentum and made the most progress have been ones backed by C-level staff. Eimear O'Connor attributes Form3's progress in this is because 'diversity and inclusion is very much at the management table'. It is seen as an integral part of the strategy rather than an add on to the agenda. She went on to say, 'gender diversity targets are very much embedded into our business plans and we are adding a more comprehensive set of diversity targets as part of our overall commitment in this space' because to change the environment real action is required.

Any programme of change within a business is more successful when sponsored by the board and executives. Too many firms have great ideas to raise the gender balance that simply don't get executed or get side-lined. If you get the budget holders on the side, it happens. Those who hold the budget need to see the business and profit impact of diversity to really back the plans.

Measurability paves the way for success as it changes goodwill and talk into reality. Some companies track the levels of women in their teams, nationalities, those who are receiving promotions, the average tenure, and how women are retained after their maternity leave. Programmes with metrics behind them are more likely to succeed. Kimberley Lewis, previous Director at Hermes Investment Management said, 'what gets reported gets done and what gets measured gets actioned, so you need targets, and you need to measure yourself against those targets'. The great news is that we are seeing many organisations across the industry becoming aware of their own demographics and the scale of change needed for gender balance or diversity. I think this is particularly powerful as the first step here is to open our eyes to how big the problem is that we face—and more importantly highlight to those who don't accept we have a problem that there is a problem to be solved.

To drive change in who and how companies hire new staff there has been a popular new trend called the 'quota system'. Many companies when hiring through external recruitment agencies, such as Harrington Starr, will demand a certain percentage of applicants who identify as female. Since there are more men in the technology space than women, 83% as of 2021, this is reflected in how many CVs are sent to the company upon application. The 'quota system' allows for a more balanced view of applicants according to gender. As a way of addressing the problem, some firms will request every one in four applicants to be female and others will request fifty-fifty parity. This encourages a better visibility of the women in the space and allows for the hiring managers to have the choice to balance their team. It is a complex point as affecting the gender imbalance in any company isn't just about hiring a lone female into a team of males. It's very much about making sure the team, the hiring manager, the culture, the people policies are all able to support and nurture that new hire and allow them to be set up for success. The decision to implement the 'quota system' puts the gender equality debate firmly on the agenda. I don't believe it solves the problem alone, but I really support the intention.

Where it really proves to be a success is when there is a manager who has the desire to make change happen and a business who wants to make the change sustainable and authentic. This is best seen in the growth of training programmes, realistic policy implementation, and internal Diversity and Inclusion Champions working in conjunction with one another. I was thrilled to speak with Eleni Vlami about exactly this. She is the Head of Account Management for Meniga, a Scandinavian founded FinTech. She explained to me that the laws and their strict enforcement in Iceland mean that there is zero gender pay gap and furthermore little gender gap in the workplace at all. Eleni said that by working for Meniga they had 'raised the bar of my expectations of equality in the workplace' and that their founding team set a standard to help, support and drive forward change in London because of their 'Scandinavian standards'. She was absolutely clear about realistic policies, how they are implemented and adhered to, 'finding a solution to make a workplace fairer doesn't have to be difficult, we start with small things, for example our 4 pm soft stop'. She went on to explain the premise of the 4PM 'soft stop' policy which means that everyone in the business know that calls and customer meetings stop at 4PM without fail to allow for those with parental or carer responsibilities to fulfil their commitments and close their day in their own time. She spoke emotively about the impact that has on the well-being of the team, no longer feeling torn or stressed because they have to excuse themselves to pick their children up from school. A wonderful example of giving your staff a 'level playing field' in their careers and supporting them in becoming the best they can be without having to sacrifice a part of themselves. Eleni didn't stop there, she continued with what she called the 'simple measure' of companywide boycotting of conferences, events, and panels where only men have been invited to speak. 'We believe in ground rules and being able to talk about this openly' and explained that their marketing team will call or email the organiser of such events to explain why there will be no Meniga presence. To Eleni this is the norm and not a bold move but a natural one.

When I spoke with Karen Rudich, in the early days of her setting up the highly successful ElementaryB she also spoke about the importance of realistic policies and their implementation, having the right policies to ensure the success of your people and therefore your company. She said, 'the new way of doing business is all about talent and the long game. That's about financial performance and if you put the right polices and processes in place to support your people and really put them at the heart of your organisation. That means having policies that are there to invest in them and retain them'. ElementaryB is an affordable cash management and working capital solution for mid-sized firms, and Karen as their Chief Executive Officer and Co-Founder brings her wealth of 20 years knowledge of investment and corporate banking specifically managing large-scale transformations. Her passion for change makes her a true realist, fighting for authentic strategy over talk and policies with substance over appearances. With her experience of building FinTechs, scaling them up and her years having worked at the giants such as Barclays, UBS Investment Bank, and BNP Paribas, Karen is able to see how no matter the size of your organisation, the future of the workplace and the success of it is about people and how they are supported. Inclusion is a huge part of this, and she spoke about the need for the re-education of staff to ensure that the real transformations in inclusion can take place.

Training is paramount and the good news is that lots of companies are now looking to educate their teams on the importance of inclusion and its correlation to their well-being, engagement, personal success, and in turn the company's success. The most commonly known training programme implemented within businesses has been that of 'unconscious bias' and helping people become 'conscious' about the way they behave and the unfair assumptions each of us make about people we deem 'different' in our lives. This penetrates deep as it is not only about recognising, understanding, and valuing people and their backgrounds, their religious, political, or cultural beliefs, instead it's about the celebration of what is deemed different.

The rise of these or similar training courses has been a step forward but again not usually successful alone. The next step is the execution of these learns and more importantly everyone who participated in them to become conscious of their internal biases and change them. It was Helen Smith, the Chief Operating Officer of Cashflows, who said back in early 2019, 'without a doubt, effective organisations are made up of differences, leaders can develop self-awareness and emotional intelligence, this is key to changing our own unconscious bias'. She made me see that these training sessions were not just about the attendance, they needed the participants to see that a fundamental difference was needed within them. Without it we will struggle in authentically creating environments where teams can be truly cohesive, skill sets can genuinely grow from one another, and people can share freely new ideas.

Alongside these lessons many companies have created entirely new roles dedicated to championing Diversity and Inclusion. It has been wonderful to see individuals tasked with rallying the rest of the company to drive actionable change. Whilst I believe it's much more about everyone being involved in inclusion, I recognise the power one individual can hold. I want to for a moment to share some of the success stories of great bosses and mentors that have made huge advancements for others. I feel this is incredibly important to share because if we were all to consider elevating those around us how far could we go?

Over a hundred of the women I have interviewed for my 'Women of FinTech' podcast series attributed their success to someone who 'gave them a chance', 'believed in them', or 'opened a door'. I find these stories so empowering and believe this is an area we must celebrate. Laura Rofe, the Strategic Partnerships Manager at PPRO said that career mentoring had 'without a doubt it helped me grow and develop my career'. She explained how having someone 'back her' and 'believe in her' allowed her to open her eyes to identify opportunities and realise potentials that she simply wouldn't have seen otherwise. Linking this directly to confidence building, Hannah Lana Preston, the Commercial Strategy Advisor of Minna Technologies shared a story about her boss, 'he never reprimanded you for your mistakes, instead he jumped in and helped get it solved'. She recalled how he would simply want to know what situation they were in, understand the reasons behind it, share the solution, and solve the problem together as a team. Hannah knows this is the root of the trust in her team and the empathy they have for one another. The power of a good boss and mentor, changes lives. Emmy Granström, the Marketing Director of SteelEye, felt just as passionately, describing herself as 'lucky in my career that I have had managers who have stood up for me and vouched for me'. When we hear about why people leave the workforce or change careers out of the sector and they say it is due to lack of support, these experiences are important to remember. Action through promotion, education without fear of reprimand when stepping out of your comfort zone and open sponsorship is needed.

Many of the women I interviewed on the podcast series described their experience of having a great mentor as a levelling of the 'playing field'. This was often highlighted by those recalling the early days of their career, remembering how important encouragement and confidence from mentors had allowed them to become the best version of themselves.

The wonderful thing I have learnt is that mentees have become mentors. Hearing from some of the mentors themselves, Katharine Wooller the Managing Director of Dacxi, said in a call to action, 'you owe it to give back, if you are lucky enough to be doing well, you have a moral obligation to give back'. The straight talker is clear about how a more cohesive team will drive a better bottom line and she believes the responsibility lies firmly in the leadership team to mentor, encourage new ideas, leverage introductions, and boost happiness at work. Celine Crawford the Chief Communications Officer of Smarkets, shares a different angle, 'I mentor people and I train them on their developmental network, and they don't really realise how many people are in their network and what is the best route to get to a specific company or industry and it's just about cultivating those relationships'. Celine likes to open people's eyes about their contacts and how to leverage them in the field. The networking we explored earlier is only at its most powerful if one knows how to make use of that network and learns to be comfortable and confident in doing so.

Nicola Breyer told me about how she gets the best out of people in her teams. She explained that for her real leadership is about adjusting to how other people like to communicate rather than imposing her own style in meetings and reviews with management. Nicola is the Chief Commercial Officer of OptioPay, a Berlin-based Fin-/AdTech which empowers consumers to create value out of their own bank data through their open banking ecosystem. Nicola has had an enormously successful career to date having worked at some of the biggest names in the space and scaling up numerous FinTechs from scratch. Her management style is about giving people the 'opportunity to grow and shine'. She believes that the success of those around her has been because, as a manager, she goes 'beyond task management, I remove obstacles, allow people to focus on their work, create networks and evolve'. Nicola was able to explain that emotive leadership did not mean being 'nice' which it is often brushed off as, instead she said allowing people to grow and become better every day means that she was forging 'business relationships about results'. The style of leadership she builds is for her team to be open-minded and have a positive relationship to learning; not only in their relevant field of expertise, but also with regard to communication, empathy, and stepping up. She also frequently asks for feedback herself and loves to observe how people become more and more frank in this over time. She concluded 'you always need mentors, it doesn't matter how old, experienced or senior you are, you need to have the confidence to reach out' a motto she lives by herself.

As with any programme of learning, people have different strengths and can therefore share different lessons. Mentoring and great bosses are about the individual doing something positive for someone else. The exciting thing about this is that it starts a waterfall effect. I have shared just a few of the strengths I see in the FinTech and the financial services technology sector, as so much action has been implemented in the pursuit of diversity and inclusion. However, we are nowhere near our goal yet and I wish to share a few of the obstacles we must remove to achieve the real change we are capable of.

8

Chasing the Tipping Point: Static for Too Long

I am incredibly passionate about the potential the FinTech industry has to change the world of work. Whilst I may be filled with positivity on this subject, the reality is in contrast to this and sadly we haven't yet fully utilised the opportunity. I have really enjoyed highlighting the challenges faced as well as showcasing the steps the industry has been making to solve the gender conundrum that every sector faces. Whilst there may have been some progress, we are simply not making a big enough dent in the issue and the metrics tell us that the gender imbalance has remained static for too long. I highlighted this in my opening chapter. As of 2021 in the UK, across all technology roles, only 17% of them are filled by women and the biggest problem with this, is that this figure has been the same for five years previously. The stats around women in FinTech are similar and again are not moving. There are many reasons for this which I will attempt to cover in the following pages. Just as I felt the need to outline and recognise the status quo in its reality, I wish to be clear on what the many people who live and breathe in this space see as the real barriers to change, despite some of the great work done and wonderful intentions that have gone hand in hand with it.

There are still some yawning gaps which rock the very foundations of all the hard work, progress and good intentions. I shared these in the previous chapter discussing 'the gaps', from societal issues to gender perceptions and pay, and without these deep foundations being addressed I fear we are spending a lot of time papering over the cracks. Sophie Theen, another award winner and 'Standout 35' of the Innovate Finance Powerlist, felt this

N. Edwards-Dashti, *FinTech Women Walk the Talk*, https://doi.org/10.1007/978-3-030-90574-3_8

lack of change 'is because we are not focussing enough on reaching the future generations'. Mainly because we haven't affected the underlying issue which she believes is to 'get rid of the banking stigma'. Sophie is the Group Chief of People and Customer Operations Officer of Akrod, another mission led FinTech seeking to transform microfinance and bring credit technology to the worlds underbanked. Not only did she identify the perception of the industry as a blocker to change, she also spoke about how crucial it is to recognise that 'it's not just about bringing more women into coding, it's actually getting the best out of women when they come into the industry'. This authenticity of environment I have been talking about is very much in support of Sophie's point. Without supporting the women we attract to the industry and getting the best for them and their career, we are perpetuating the problem. The task isn't to attract more women into positions in the industry, but instead to make the industry more attractive to women. A subtle difference in vernacular but a huge difference in execution. Nim Haas, the Founder of TechFuse, felt the real issue was simply lack of action following good theory. For example, she questioned, 'what are you actually doing out of your office to implement diversity? How many attend a panel or talk and go back to the Founder or Chief Executive Officer and ask for change to happen?' Nim has inspired me to be as action orientated as I am, in every talk I host, roundtable I run, or panel I speak on, without fail I will remember this sentiment and use it to drive actionable outcomes and pledges for change. Nim, again was one to highlight that change isn't happening and won't happen unless we focus on the deep foundations of the problem, from environment, to action, to feeling safe enough in your team to ask for action, or better more, initiate it yourself.

As I explained previously, this 'all talk and no action' parody is very much a driver behind my phrase 'walk the talk' to draw attention to those who follow discussion with action and to entice more to the movement.

Sarah Carver, Head of Global Digital at Delta Capita, said to this point, there is the widespread 'realisation that talk is cheap and time has come for action in lots of different areas of diversity and I think talk is no longer deemed acceptable by society and action is what's required'. Another clear demand for actionable change. Whilst I really appreciate the realisation that we must do more is widespread, I am cognizant that we must be clear on exactly what that means should we wish to drive this change.

It was Seema Khinda Johnson who was the first to raise this with me when we met in 2018 and helped me escalate my own journey of the 'how'. I had the pleasure of inviting her into my offices in early 2020 to record our podcast. She shared her career journey of Co-Founding Nuggets, a payment and identity business helping to protect customer data. Her point was similar to those afore mentioned; 'what's been great over the last couple of years is that a light has been shone on the fact that we need to do more but you aren't really seeing that in reality. Although there's lots of initiatives that have been set up, lots of organisations are trying to own the conversations around this - I don't think there has been real tangible results or outcomes from these'. She identified that there was a gap between policies introduced and procedures that take place day to day. I see this often, where businesses have certain policies around unconscious bias or hiring strategies, but the reality ends up being different.

Miia Paavola of PLEO called it out as well. She is currently a Product Manager at PLEO, a company dedicated to smart cards for businesses. When demanding equality in the workplace said that it was simply a choice to make it happen or not and that the biggest barrier is those who have the control of hiring. In discussing how this should be improved, she spoke of the 'look harder concept' and summarised 'If you haven't found diversity for the company you haven't tried hard! There are so many powerful and amazing women in the industry so you can't say they aren't out there. If they are not in your network, you need to look beyond it'. It isn't complex if we tackle it right and address the real issues. Where we have struggled is that we have chosen to talk and not act. As businesses, we still haven't connected success with inclusion, revenue with engagement or staff working in psychological safety with profits despite all that has been written about it. I have seen implementation of numerous policies in hopes of quick wins, when everything I have learnt tells me that to authentically impact this problem it will take a more longer-term approach and more importantly a more all-encompassing approach.

When considering the success of the award ceremonies I spoke of previously, Joanne Dewar, Chief Executive Officer of Global Processes Services, has been a major proponent of increasing recognition and confidence. She had also been clear that she had implemented training, policy, and well-defined procedures to improve communication, inclusion, and equity across the business. She was one of the first people I talked to about my pregnancy with my first baby and she helped me to understand I would need to decide what I wanted for my career and build my own policies and procedures. She helped me in my understanding, that because every person has different wants, needs, desires, and circumstances we cannot identify one 'silver bullet' in the pursuit of real inclusion in our workplaces.

All of the fantastic work individuals and businesses have been pursuing sadly doesn't make a dent alone and evidence of this cannot be clearer than seeing three high-profile women during the course of the end of 2020 and early 2021 join then leave their C-level positions within the FinTech and financial services community. These three women had only started their roles within the year previous and it begs the question, what was the real reason they left? Sadly, many will assume COVID-19 related, when armed with more information it had become clear that ingenuous culture was at the root. Whether businesses win awards or not, if they don't have the people and culture agreeing to the inclusion policies and procedures then the whole premise is undermined.

Kenzy Goodwin, Partner at Finceler8, spoke about how we can keep working on bringing women to the industry but questioned the 'leaky pipeline' highlighting again the problem of losing women from the industry after only a few years. She raised the points that previously the leaky pipeline was attributed to family commitments and women being perceived as the main caregivers. Kenzy spoke about how women entering the industry 'must be supported and made visible so that others can feel connected, and they can feel that they belong'. She went on to explain similarly to the 'no silver bullet' that we need to work together across the industry to do more together to connect men and women in similar roles and help them forge career networks to allow for wider support. This sense of belonging is a really important theme that has proved difficult to build without going back to schools and universities to set the foundations.

Kelly Read-Parish, the Chief Operating Officer of Credit Kudos, spoke of her personal experience with belonging, 'I have a lasting memory walking into my university's engineering computer lab and immediately noticing I was the only female in the room, and how that made me feel'. She went on to share what it was like to build her career in finance where she was often the only woman in the room. In tackling this she felt the media has a big part to play 'in changing stereotypes of what an engineer or someone who goes into banking looks like to make it more inclusive to women, people of colour, and individuals from different backgrounds'.

With this in mind I am encouraged every time I see the EDF Energy adverts on UK television. They have made a marked effort to exhibit a diverse number of their job roles with diverse people as incumbents. Energy companies similar to the financial sector, face a lot of stigma in the world today and for EDF Energy to have adverts regularly showcasing diversity of people, in a range of roles, on a mission to achieve zero carbon electricity will no doubt encourage people to their company and the wider industry. The simplicity of letting people see what roles are available and people they can identify with in those roles is really empowering, especially when reaching out to the next generation. The issue that Kelly raises is of perception and our lack of ability to make enough of a dent in the negative perceptions that exist. The FinTech industry isn't acknowledged near enough for its work in serving the under-served, or educating the underbanked, or contributing to the world of green finance, perhaps because not enough of this is done or that simply the more traditional ways of working still supersede the new. The work being done to educate school children and entice them to the world of technology isn't driving the change and all the career fairs at universities again aren't reaching the results sought nearly as much as they could. Sangeetha Narasimham of Mambu, a massive believer in role modelling for next generation, felt the missing piece could be that 'If women aspire to get into payments, we mustn't forget to show them there is a starting point for it and not just have them look at C level women'. A very valid point and one we see Vanessa Vallely tackling year on year with her Rising Star Awards in the wearethecity.com commu-nity. Vanessa's community building was the first to bridge this gap and allows for relatable peers to be celebrated in the industry. The problem remains, and the issue that stands for me is that the industry and people within are making some great efforts, but some of these aren't achieving the results because a piece of the puzzle has been overlooked.

It was Joanne Dewar's comments yet again which resonated with me. She had been recalling when she won an incredibly sought after and prestigious award in 2019, the Payments Power 10. She described the win as 'the first time I've been recognised among the "big boys" as opposed to being recog-nised as the women in payments'. She went on to share that whilst all awards are important, she felt that it was 'even more important to make that jump to be seen to be on an equal footing'. So yet again we see great strives forward, but it can fail to reach the tipping point. The awards, the events, the sympo-siums, the webinars all make a dent but if these are only women events, we are missing the bigger picture and that incredibly important 'equal footing'. This is not to say the 'women in x' awards don't achieve our goals; my point is we need to drive these initiatives further. Johanna Maria Leiner, the VP of Compliance, Governance and Ethics at Paysafe Group, made me think about going further in our work and reaching that 'tipping point' when she highlighted that 'lots of companies have one female board member and they think they have done enough. We need to have more and show how women are doing it and how they cope with family'. Herein lies the static reality. The drive for authentic inclusion will encapsulate a lot more than hiring a set number of females into a business. Every business will need to forge the right culture and environment for this to be sustainable and think about the challenges certain demographics face.

Looking at working mums, we must consider that there will be different demands on them than single people, men with a support structure at home, or people with no caregiving responsibilities. When we think about the equity building in our environments, it is paramount to understand each individual and their specific needs. Only then can we explore whether the business is supporting them to be the best version of themselves at work or whether the business is hindering them. Societally we still have a long way to go, with the perception of women in the workplace as leaders, as working mothers, as successful businesspeople. Historically these perceptions have stopped women from having the opportunities. More recently, the mountain can be conquered but there is a steeper route to its peak for women in companies who refuse to acknowledge the equity needed to build a gender-balanced sustainable workforce. In talks with Patricia Salume, the other Co-Founder of VeeLoop and VHelp, she spoke about how equity in a business is created. Having achieved a successful funding round whilst heavily and visibly pregnant, she felt that the realities of returning to work needed to be made clearer in all workplaces. She spoke about options for returning mothers that included phased or staged returns, flexible hours, breastfeeding considerations, where that will happen in the office, and what happens when someone has been up all night with a baby with colic. Patricia encourages people across the industry to talk 'about this more and enable people to have a better way to return to work and manage both work and family' to be a success in both. There's no point in saying you will hire returning mothers or support women returning to work when in fact they won't be made to feel valued, welcomed, or psychologically safe. She also highlighted the hugely important issue of talent retention, if genuine support is offered to people at whatever stage in their life and empathy is shown then people are less likely to leave, she concluded only then will people be able to 'grow in their job and move on with their lives'. There are many points that I particularly relate to, having recently embarked on my motherhood journey. In the few late months of 2020, before the UK went into their second lockdown, I commuted to the office a few days a week and it was absolutely imperative to me that I had a private room where I felt safe to breast pump whilst working. If at any point I had felt someone would walk into this safe space or that I couldn't be sat in a comfy chair with a raised table for my laptop (so I could continue working) I would have been discouraged from going into the office as I wouldn't have been able to work whilst I prepared my baby's milk. Feeling that there was no stigma attached to where I was going when I left the office sales floor and that I had my own private fridge, made the world of difference to me feeling welcomed back and given a 'level playing field'. The thought of me having to hide in office toilets whilst pumping and unable to work, losing precious minutes of the working day simply would have been an exit for me. One woman told me of the lack of authentic inclusion in her workplace saying that if her child had an emergency, the culture was of irritation rather than concern when she had to leave a meeting or rush out of the office. Another told of her co-workers calling her a 'part-timer' in a derogatory fashion because she left the office at 4 to pick up her children. She made it clear that whilst her co-workers would spend their evenings in the pubs she would log back into work as her children slept. These are just a few of the realities and having Diversity, Equity, and Inclusion agendas don't provide the policy nor the procedures nor the more important acceptance that's needed to turn this into a reality.

Interestingly, in talks with Hannah Preston of Minna Technologies, she reminded me that, 'lots of women ask me, "can you have it all? What are the trade-offs and sacrifices you have to make?"' Hannah is a super successful female on the FinTech scene working in an incredibly high powered position and she instils confidence in all who she mentors and supports through their careers. She is adamant that 'you can balance a career and motherhood but you have to be realistic, and you must know your own limitations and what your priorities are'. She helped me upon my return to the office full time as she shared how she had exclusively breast fed her boy for his first year despite returning to work after 5 weeks. For Hannah, having her son was when her 'life began' and she said about it, 'I knew that I could make a difference in this world to make it a better place for my boy and for me, it wasn't an option to not pursue that'. Hannah is incredibly driven by technology for good, passionate about paying it forward, and strives to serve the underserved in her day-to-day work, whilst being a brilliant mum to her boy. We talk often about the 'can you have it all debate?' and rather than answer this question we ask why in society men aren't asked this? Why aren't we supporting women more to have the same in which men have, a family, a social life, and a career? When you pause for a moment and ponder that, it is easy to see unconscious bias in all of us and the limitations we put on ourselves and the relationships we all have in our households, in our friendships and in our workplaces.

Ioanna Stanegloudi raised this too when she spoke about founding her business, Finclude. She believes that women are not supported enough in their post maternity return to the workplace. She highlighted that upon return too many women feel as if they have been side-lined, demoted, and as if they no longer can contribute to the workplace. Culturally she called for action in the workplace where on top of extended or shared maternity and paternity policies, there was a recognition piece around the value new mothers can add, 'we need their input in business and we need to show them that they can be both and actually, be whatever they want'. This disbelief in women in general and then even more so following any time out of the workplace must be ended. Whilst I see many companies now embarking on the journey to encourage women back after maternity, I see little around educating managers and team members about the new parameters in which they return. Discussing this with her made me think again of falling short of the tipping point.

It was Leda Glyptis, Chief Client Officer of 10x Banking, who raised a connected issue when she spoke about all the effort gone into training without addressing the deep-rooted societal perceptions of genders. She said, 'gendered leadership hurts us all, we make it hard for men to be empathetic and for women to be strong'. Looking at societal perceptions of genders in the workplace the traditional way of leading was as Leda described, hard-nosed, results driven, non-emotional, and all associated with male traits. When women have exhibited similar traits they are questioned, and when men exhibit the more traditionally identified female traits of collaboration, empathy, and listening, they are seen as weak. She had concluded that 'we need a world where empathy and strength are not seen as mutually exclusive'. It is exactly these limitations that prevent us from reaching the tipping point. All the good work needs this further context and analysis to make an impact. Furthermore, when these traits cross the archaic gender borders, we need environments where everyone is supported, and the naysayers are called out for their behaviours.

Working with people and investing in their future success was brought up in my conversation with Eimear O'Connor, the Chief Operating Officer of Form3. Eimear has grown her business with a people-first and people investment focus. She felt passionately about not just doing the training or having the weekly reviews and meetings. Culturally she outlined that she needed to go a step further by 'giving people space to grow in their success and ultimately fail as well'. Introducing me to the term 'supported failure' Eimear spoke about her learns from managing and building up both men and women in her career. She highlighted that 'a lot of the female talent I have worked with focus on the "not perfect" outcomes and this can very easily turn to the negative rather than the positive things that were achieved and the learning experience for next time'. Working on changing these views and creating an environment where being 'brave' is key and failure is equated to learning has brought the authenticity to what she is trying to achieve. It wasn't a task where she only focused on women and how women behave, instead she looked at the environments in which she worked and how she could make them more accustomed to learning without a fear of failure and actually reframing that failure as part of the learning journey. For Eimear, 'any aspiring leader needs to get comfortable that a bit of failure and learning how to grow from that is really important and that the support structures are in place to allow for that'.

Taking this concept of failure and Eimear's point that when women review themselves, they can often focus on what they haven't achieved over what they have, I was reminded of my conversation with Dagmara Aldridge, the Chief Operating Officer of Zumo. Dagmara is leading the charge with a career history of constantly stretching out of her comfort zone and trying out new things despite the fear of potential failure. She felt that this obsession many women have with the imperfect is deeply rooted in our childhoods saying, 'girls are brought up to be perfect and boys are brought up to take risks' and as a 'little girl I remember being told by family members and teachers to be less; less loud, less curious and less demanding and that can be so damaging to your confidence'. It is no wonder with this in mind, another societal expectation and base line that so many women suffer from imposter syndrome in their careers. Interestingly, the work on imposter syndrome that has been done has been focused on the individual who lacks that confidence rather than the environment or company culture to lift that person up.

Mel Tsiaprazis, Chief Commercial Officer of BitStamp, spoke about her drive in the business to 'nurture talent and nurture the culture so people can continue to improve themselves and ultimately to deliver the best work of their careers'. Within this she warned that the more senior you become 'the louder the imposter voice kicks in' and therefore the solution to it can never just be a training session or review, but instead it is found within the entire culture and ethos of a business. In conclusion, she spoke of continually and consistently supporting everyone's confidence in an empathetic way through authentic celebration, correct attribution of credit, open forums for debate, and actively seeking out diversity of opinion. Emmanuelle Mathey, the Co-Chief Risk Officer for Wealth Management and Group Head of Credit Risk at Schroders, drew upon this unsolved problem too, beseeching with the audience of our podcast, saying, 'don't self-censor'. She wanted us to discuss the sheer volume of women who won't apply for the job, the promotion or discuss the fact that they are way overdue a pay rise. She also raised the point about working environments needing to be 'two ways', having the individuals reaching out and asking alongside the business being an environment where people felt they could ask. Another perspective comes from Alia Cooper, the EMEA Head of Compliance Network at HSBC, when she recalled her career journey, she spoke about imposter syndrome and not just from a female viewpoint, she spoke about what she had learnt about imposter syndrome across other minorities in the workplace. Her view was that there hasn't been and still isn't enough support for people who suffer from this 'feeling of not quite belonging' and that 'it is our problem to solve'. Alia bravely admitted she now can see that imposter syndrome is something she has suffered from throughout her career. For her it has become her driver for the vast amounts of mentoring she does. Alia has set up workshops and committees to broaden the understand and awareness of disabilities and mental health across HSBC to action this saying 'It's societies problem and we all have a part to play, we cannot allow people to feel like they don't have someone to help them'.

When I spoke with Cindy van Niekerk about her funding journey, I felt I learnt a lot about myself and how I need to behave in the workplace and with my clients, should I wish to hit my tipping point and make a real difference to workplace inclusion for the long term. Cindy's sheer enthusiasm and drive to learn through every experience makes it a certainty that she will succeed with her new business, Umazi. She was driven by years of working in the regulatory space and seeing huge inefficiencies in due diligence and the lack of care around it. Her proposition is clearly needed across the industry but at the point of writing this, Cindy was applying for funding and had pitched over 80 times in a four month period. She shared her learns telling me that she had to get comfortable on stage, then to speak 'like a Chief Executive Officer,' and then to seek feedback. Cindy had invested in a pitch coach and was really clear about how she was planning on handling the colossal funding gap. Firstly, she said, 'you give life to what you give energy to so whenever you get a no, ask why it's a no and only take the critique you can build on'. Secondly, she spoke about how she learnt to understand that 'you will always have to justify the existence of your company' and to get used to it. This something I have taken with me from the conversation, I am often reminded of this sentiment when talking about my job, what I am attempting to achieve and how I am doing it. The work Cindy has done to share her learns and instil confidence in others makes the industry and the culture of the industry more welcoming, and the perception of it is that much more penetrable. It has been brilliant to hear so many of the women featured in this book say that they will themselves become angel investors to tackle the gap, and we see so many venture capital firms grow in their female presence, but the funding problem remains as the worst statistical gap I will mention in the entirety of the book. We still face a huge challenge in tackling the funding gap and the confidence in women Founders. Which lends the question, why don't we strive towards this tipping point where real change happens? Why are we spending time on good actions but either not the right ones or not taking it far enough? What is it that gets in the way?

As I have shown there have been so many policies that haven't been taken far enough, then we have seen actions focused on one area rather than the ecosystem itself and more often than not we see actions for actions' sake. Too many businesses in trying to find a solution miss the point all together, especially when they focus on their image over the issue itself.

I invited Sonya Barlow to speak on a panel I was hosting for the Diversity Network, an organisation I regularly support in their events. I have known Sonya for a number of years through the extraordinarily unique network she founded called Like Minded Females. I have both attended and spoken at events she has held and found it a brilliant network of people from all sorts of industries, who seek to embetter themselves in their career and have come together to think differently in safety. During this particular panel we debated authentic inclusion and Sonya said, 'if you have the right skills or people, any business can call themselves a diversity and inclusion champion if they copyright it the right way'. She spoke about the title-grabbing and badge-wearing across the industry where companies label themselves advocates but in reality, don't follow through with inclusive habits. She went on to call out the damaging behaviours of judges at awards who are not 'representative and see a 2% increase in a statistic as worthy of an award'. This is a genuine problem where businesses win an award and think their task is complete. Sonya's stressed that often businesses who are not practising inclusion have fabulous marketing departments who know exactly how to write a brilliant award application. Knowing that the inconsistencies exist, her businesses are dedicated to building that authentic inclusion within culture, strategy, environment, and people for the long run. The practices she often sees betray the entire movement.

As previously highlighted, Nim Haas, the award-winning FinTech marketeer said the same of panels themselves questioning 'what is the point if you don't turn it into action?' Since hearing her say this I always drive home the message that if anyone is attending a talk of mine, a roundtable I have hosted or a panel discussion, they must take with them a pledge of action to make that time invested worthwhile. Nim's words ring in my mind, 'change doesn't happen with just panels, change happens if you give the people listening the right tools and understanding of how they can implement it'.

Similarly, barriers to action can come in the form of senior leaders not being part of the journey. When, as an example, we look at training around how men and women generally communicate and the appreciation of everyone's communication differences, all it takes is one of the managers in the business to undermine someone for stepping out of their traditional gendered characteristics and the whole education exercise is negated. There have been a number of examples of this across the industry where an entire business has taken part in unconscious bias training, only for a C-level member of staff to brush off its importance and undermine the whole exercise. Similarly, as discussed, mentoring makes a huge difference no doubt, but actually the problem we face isn't to make women more successful it is actually in making them viewed as successful as they are. Ultimately without C-level support the training won't work and without altering the perception of women in the workplace, mentoring can only take us so far.

When the focus is on the wrong thing, people feel it is ingenuine, they don't see change happening and merely don't want to get involved. Ritesh Jain, the Founder of Infynit, called it 'diversity fatigue' when he explained how people will opt out of good initiatives if you have lost their confidence previously. Sarah Carver, the Global Head of Digital at Delta Capita, was an example of this when she admitted that in the past she hadn't 'got involved in initiatives as they have felt so tick box and I was a little sceptical'. Now an avid driver of building genuine policies, instilling visible role models, and following up by building a gender-balanced team around her, Sarah knows the importance of authentic actions. This scepticism is often seen when businesses implement the 'quota system' without any further protocols. In discussing this earlier I explained the premise and the intention of hiring managers gaining better visibility of applicants identifying as each gender. This is done through a set of instructions to their recruitment agencies when hiring and requesting CVs so that they, in theory will receive a better gender balance. My concern with only using a 'quota system' is that businesses put the onus on external parties to solve an everybody problem. It does not address the all-important environment I have repeatedly spoken about. It does not address the bias within the hiring managers, it doesn't drive psychological safety across the team, nor does it give credibility to why inclusion is better for all.

Suresh Vaghjiani, the award-winning Chief Executive Officer of Clowd 9, said 'I don't believe it's the right thing' when we discussed the rise in the 'quota system'. He felt that although the intention was good and raised awareness of the topic it didn't take it far enough as inclusion goes beyond race or gender. He addressed the real barrier to inclusion when he admitted, 'people go for what they think are the safe options when hiring', often people that seem similar to them and the way they work, not mothers, not carers and 'no amount of quotas will change that'. He believed vehemently that we have to address the hearts and minds of hiring managers to help them understand that difference will make their teams better and their businesses stronger. He spoke about protection measures being implemented to hold managers accountable for their hiring and decisions around hiring. Essentially the 'quota system' needs scaffolding to be truly successful and reach anywhere near the tipping point we are striving towards.

From my recruitment perspective, its key to appreciate that when businesses reach out to recruitment agencies it's because they have a need to hire and normally that need is urgent or at least has some sort of time pressure on it, hence reaching out for external support on it. Putting the inclusion agenda under a time pressure of a hire does not set it up for success. We know in the technology scene of the UK today only 17% of it is made up of females, therefore if a hiring manager was to see 100 applicants it is likely they will bump in 83 men and 17 women. Put simply they are more likely to see a man that can do the job before a woman and in turn hire what they see first. This is one of the many points of failure in the current recruitment process most of the industry subscribes to. The recruitment industry has a huge part to play to affect change. Interestingly, where on the one hand FinTech is seen as adaptable, changing, and agile, many of the recruitment practices are outdated. For example, businesses still will advertise their vacancies with bullet points and demands for a litany of skills just like they would have done 30 years ago. Even though many have made the step to making their job descriptions gender neutral, this isn't going to make all the difference alone. They may have good intentions but without being agile enough to transform entirely how they recruit, change will be difficult to happen. These realities of time pressures and getting business critical skills into the company, and that individual making a quick impact often supersedes the desire to drive inclusion and sadly we see the topic disappear time and time again into luxury items on a companywide agenda.

Often in searching for a solution we see great suggestions that sound right in theory but fail in practice. The biggest problem here is when people overlook the failure and convince themselves they are solving the problem. An example of this came from Cecil Adjalo, who spoke alongside me at a panel for Finastra. He wanted to share an experience around anonymous employer surveys, saying 'My employer sent around a company survey we all had to fill in anonymously about our experience at work. One of the questions was about my race and another was my department. At the time I was the only black person in my department so I skipped the race question because they would have known it was me'. He did not feel safe in the environment to answer questions around inclusion, diversity, communication, debate, and innovation. Cecil is a thought leader in the space and is an executive director for a community interest company helping Founders from underrepresented backgrounds build and scale start-ups from just an idea. The faith in anonymous surveys actually being anonymous is limited and furthermore the point Cecil raised was that if you are the only minority in a group filling in a survey, it will be obvious which one you wrote because you will exhibit a diversity of thought. This example is one I have used to highlight that however much work is done, without the foundation of building an environment where people feel they are psychologically safe to call out injustice, improvements and invention, then we don't make the step forwards.

In talks with Alex Ford, the VP of Product and Marketing at Encompass Corporation, another understandable point was raised about businesses wanting to tackle inclusion authentically getting overwhelmed by the level of change needed. A lot of businesses simply don't know where to start. She implored the audience in her podcast saying, 'inaction is also a decision, you must take the first step and iterate from there'. This inaction can lead to far bigger problems where companies are losing credibility for how they are treating their staff and in turn struggling to meet project demands because of lack of staff because no one wants to work for them. Lindsey Jayne, the VP of Product for a FinTech called Yoco, called this out when she said, 'why would we need someone praying in the stairwell or breast pumping in the toilet to realise we aren't inclusive?' Yoco is an African technology company that builds tools and services to help small businesses get paid, run their business better and grow. Their whole ethos is about understanding the perspective of their customer. This was reflected in her comments when she said, 'It's not ok to ask people who haven't been thought of to demand to be included, we need to do the hard work for them'.

This message is one that I hear time and time again. Felicitas Coulibaly, the Global Head of Inside Sales at Mambu, was another person to identify this problem saying, 'we can't always rely on black people to educate you on racism and women who are being harassed at work to educate you on sexism'. She called out managers, peers, and business leaders saying for anyone to be successful in the world of business they need to 'actively work to educate themselves'. Felicitas raised an important point, that people need to want to be educated to fully reap the benefits of the numerous training sessions that have been implemented across the space. Pulling on this thread I can see very clearly why so little action is garnered after these training sessions, because we need to open everyone's eyes that inclusion is inclusion for all and for the benefit of us all.

I find myself asking people within the industry about the last time they spoke up about a bias they witnessed or put forward a colleague who they saw had been overlooked for a promotion. There are numerous ways we can address all of what prevents us from authentically inclusive environments and lots of action points that can encourage everyone to take part. Ritesh Jain, the Founder of Infynit, identified these actions as a step beyond having a diverse workforce, saying 'Diversity alone doesn't work - you need inclusivity' and he went on to describe this as a culture where everyone feels valued and free to be themselves because you have created the environment to be one of support and nurturing. When I asked how we can create such an environment he explained that 'empathy sits at the core' and that can be encouraged by treating people fairly by instilling this through regulation to ensure everyone is appreciated.

Identifying what this sense of value and appreciation can be is clearly outlined in the example of Zoe Newman, the US Managing Director at Capital on Tap, and her phenomenal career trajectory. She felt companies need to put faith in the growth of their staff and invest in their Careers. She explained how her own team has 'really pushed me to try new things and go outside of my comfort zone'. She went on to explain how Capital on Tap has grown and the opportunities that its growth have given her; 'it's the FinTech start up approach, we say we need to do something like investigate a new country, so we look around and ask who in our team right now can grab hold of that?' In describing her own career trajectory in the business, she spoke passionately about the loyalty this approach has bread for her, the company had trusted her, and she in turn trusted them. She has received multiple promotions and has worked in a number of roles where she has been encouraged to try new things without fear of failure.

A large part of the solution I am taking us towards is through eradicating this 'fear of failure' by building psychological safety in the environment, having policies backed by management and followed through with procedure. It all revolves around helping each individual, whoever they are and whatever their background, become the best they can be. I think of Monica Millares, the Head of Product Experience at Big Pay, when I talk about real psychological safety, where you feel totally free to showcase your unique self. Big Pay, like Monica, is on a mission to challenge traditional banking by making banking accessible to everyone, no matter their age, occupation or nationality, through their customer focused money app. Monica is passionate about sharing your ideas freely to allow for the best-in-class innovations. She is an advocate for positive reinforcements that your differences are your strengths, and she says inclusion is about learning and erasing the 'stress around not knowing how to do something'. Instead let's build environments where you show your true self including your vulnerabilities, so others feel free to join you. She argues that everyone should be open about their learns through their career journey so that no one individual seems like the finished article. Instead she calls for everyone to be passionate about their own personal growth to pave the way for others to do so in safety. To reach the tipping point we need to address these hurdles I have been highlighting and in the next chapter, I wish to outline exactly how we can bring all this knowledge together to do that in a sustainable way.

9

Moving the Needle: Action

Moving the needle on this topic is our challenge. Getting results that last and reflect the gender balance of society for the good of the team, business, industry, and wider economy is our goal. Whilst many excellent initiatives have 'tipped' the scale, I have spoken in depth about our failure to reach the tipping point. In this chapter I wish to outline the key factors that will enable any industry to do so but specifically the financial services, FinTech and technology sectors with the huge opportunity we have in our ability to drive change, solve problems and achieve true diversity of thought. So far, I have celebrated the positive steps, then the reasons why they have failed to reach a tipping point and now I seek to show how we do. It is my overwhelming belief that to drive any real movement towards our goal we need to be honest with ourselves about fixing the very foundations of the problem.

These foundations range from societal barriers including perceptions of gender and perceptions of the industry, building psychological safety and the biggest one of all, leaders within business deciding that this is imperative to their success and therefore choosing to make it happen. There is a plethora of factors which I will discuss on top of these issues, but the basics are where I wish to start.

I remember three conversations that really stood out for me and got me questioning the real root of why we haven't reached our goal and what needs to happen. Each of these people spoke so candidly and made me think immediately that we simply need to make the choice to make this happen, not as a 'nice to have' or an 'add on' to a strategic agenda but to ensure it is front and

© The Author(s), under exclusive license to Springer Nature
Switzerland AG 2022
N. Edwards-Dashti, *FinTech Women Walk the Talk*,
https://doi.org/10.1007/978-3-030-90574-3_9

centre. Jamie Howard, the CTO of Capital on Tap, a business I have celebrated a number of times for its culture and people focused values is another
person who raised the point that 'the best debates come from diverse teams'.
He went on to say that the gender imbalance in the industry is 'a problem
that is well known, but it's not a problem that people know how to solve'. He
went on to talk through all the work that he and the rest of the team at
Capital on Tap do to address the gender imbalance by making their business as attractive and successful as possible. He shared how they are investing
in each and every staff member to feel supported yet challenged, offering
them flexibility whilst driving people to be more productive, spending time
building people's careers and celebrating them for their differences. With all
of his solutions to the challenge, the point that rang in my ears was that, in an
industry so steeped in solving problems we wish to solve why do we struggle
with this problem? The next conversation I won't forget was that with the
straight talker, Sylvia Carrasco, the Chief Executive Officer of Goldex. She
said in her podcast 'talking is definitely important but now is the time to
start doing' and we all need to take part in this 'doing'. Yet again I ask myself
why aren't we all 'doing' more? Why do we continue having the conversation
without turning it into the positive actions of reaching out to universities,
hiring more women from outside the industry, cross training them, and then
investing into the women we have, so they don't leave?

Another person who was so clear about the actions needed was Iraide Ruiz,
the Technology Manager and Technology Diversity Champion at IG. IG is
one of the global leaders in online trading, well known and established in
1974 as the world's first financial spread betting firm they have for many
years been at the forefront of technology innovation. Iraide unapologetically
said 'if you want more women in your technology teams, go and get them',
seek out women with technology skills, train them up, cross train from other
industries, open your minds to identifying potential rather than expecting
the skill set you need to be ready made for you. I absolutely concur with this
exacting level of commitment to the solution but again it makes me more
acutely aware of what the real problem is.

As an industry we continue to say to one another that we 'will think about
it' rather than invest in this level of change. Having spoken to hundreds of
Chief Executive Officers about the lack of gender balance in the sector, I have
come to realise that one of the main reasons we miss the very foundations of
change needed is because the heads of these businesses, the founders, and or
the C-Level members of staff haven't connected the notion of success, profits,
revenue, valuations, and customer success with inclusion.

The reality of the financial services and FinTech community is that there is a huge demand for talent. As the sector gains more traction and customer bases continue to grow, businesses need to become more attractive in their working environments to ensure they can grow at the pace their product's success demands. Aysun Ahi, the Chief People Officer of OpenPayd spoke about the realities of a fast-growing FinTech.

OpenPayd is dedicated to improving access to, and quality of, the payment and banking services available to businesses within the digital economy. As such they have built their team across Europe and are incredibly committed to having people who not only want to join but want to stay for the long term. Aysun said, 'we compete hard for the best talent, we have a culture where people develop; they have a healthy work life balance, they are empowered'. She went on to explain how she and the leadership team ensure all their staff are supported, whoever they are and from whatever background by explaining that 'diversity and inclusion is not just a trendy expression to use, it requires real action to ensure people are respected and recognised for their unique perspectives and contributions'. This use of 'trend' is an important one as we have seen time and time again where companies have put 'diversity' on their strategic agenda, not because they authentically wish to achieve it but merely for the kudos in following the latest trend. To realise the true power of diversity and inclusion, companies need to embrace it wholeheartedly and implement it fully throughout the organisation.

Sadly, I have seen some driven by the possibility of an ingenuine award to promote their business or because they feel diversity should be part of the conversation but are not really committed to reaching it.

Liza Russell makes the diversity-success connection really simple. She is the Chief Operating Officer of Inbotiqa, and said that 'I'm involved heavily in recruitment, and I drive that inclusive mix so that everybody brings something special to the team'. Going further she spoke about how right from the inception of the business she ensured diversity and being inclusive with it was in their 'DNA' and they attribute their continuing success to such a foundation. Dagmara is another connector. As the Chief Operating Officer of Zumo she has taken it upon herself and her team to drive the business successes through their attraction of people from all backgrounds. For her, the connection between inclusion and success is clear, 'diversity and difference drives creativity, innovation, different perspectives, increases problem solving and improves engagement. This leads to more representative solutions for wider society and that in turn translates to higher engagement and higher revenues'. Celine Crawford, Chief Communications Officer of Smarkets gets involved in people focused strategy and authentic inclusion policies and procedures because 'you are creating ambassadors and creating champions for your brand'. These examples are of only a handful of women in the industry who are hands-on with this challenge and they are so because they never doubt the connection between inclusion and success and this belief drives their actions that follow.

Many organisations are seeing the light and committing to actions with robust outcomes. A brilliant example of this is in the sudden growth of 'Diversity and Inclusion Committees' across numerous firms in 2021 that consist of mixed gender and seniority. I have loved being in contact with so many of the individuals running these committees to talk through where they should start and what, in my opinion are the 'high impact first steps'. The beauty of what I have been seeing is the contribution from C Level as well as middle management and that more men are getting involved to make their businesses better places to work from a diversity and inclusion perspective. Some have introduced monetary incentives and bonus schemes to reward those who lead inclusively explaining that leading inclusively is leading successfully and should be rewarded. Payal Raina is the Founder of FinTech B2B Marketing Community and the Global Head of Marketing at Torstone, a post-trade technology innovation business. Payal is a massive believer in departmental collaboration in the form of such committees, saying that 'we as leaders shouldn't wait for others to make a change but through collaboration across the business nurture people's differences'.

She spoke in her podcast about how Torstone boasts in their employees over thirty different nationalities. But, more importantly, they have created a culture where these individuals want to learn from one another's perspectives. As a growing FinTech, 'we are transparent that diversity is key to business success'. As such, they encourage everyone to refer new members to the company, building psychological safety. She continued to say that she aims to drive the diversity initiative forward through her FinTech B2B Marketing community platform as well so FinTech marketers can play their role in making the needle move.

Michelle Johnson, the Head of UK and Ireland for Fexco Payments and FX, a FinTech specialising in card payments and foreign exchange, was able to boast some incredible wins when sharing her work as part of the Fexco Women in Payments (WIP) Steering Committee. A global business that began thirty years ago out of a tiny village in Ireland, Fexco's WIP has '20% male allies and 60% representation from global locations' allowing for true diversity of thought and opinion to be shared and considered. She says 'it's not just about women, it's about payments and innovation and ensuring that we are maximising relationships and revenues' because we are inclusive and including everyone.

These committees are turning talk into action and having various seniority levels within them makes an immediate impact as backing from the top of any organisation is a key element in driving any strategic change. More and more companies are understanding that inclusion is not about potential awards but instead the unglamourous day in day out cultural architecture that will allow for people to become the best they can be and therefore make the business the best it can be. It will take time and will need policies backed up by procedures that take place and everyone taking part. This will only start on the right footing if business heads, and C-Level staff are seen to drive and implement these changes first. If the key players of any business have diverse perspectives or demand more diverse perspectives to propel their success forward, then anything is possible. Without this drive all the 'good' actions are built on quicksand. Kimberley Abbott, the Founder and Chief Executive Officer of Vested Impact said 'It's not about more women at the table it's about women at the table with a voice that counts, that's heard' and who better to listen but those who have the power to make the change happen. Helen Smith, the Chief Operating officer of Cashflows concurred, 'The only way we change the organisational environment, which directly impacts our ability to improve performance and results, is to put the right leaders in place', those who will make the connection between inclusion and success. She went on to demand that we need leaders who will build and create the environment where people can genuinely be authentic and be themselves so you 'get diversity, you get that richness of thought and background' in turn allowing your business to thrive.

When we share these messages of leaders connecting inclusion with success across the industry, we do a world of good for changing the perception of the space. When leaders show the way and change their behaviours it automatically gives permission for everyone else within the business to do so. The image of FinTech, financial services, and technology is one we have covered in detail and our ability to showcase to the wider world how far we have come on our 'inclusion journeys' is imperative in changing the negative connotations that surround working in the industry. Jamie Howard, the Chief Technology Officer of Capital on Tap was one of many to say, 'it does need society to raise awareness of the sector and the type of work we do and problems we solve so that girls growing up aspire to be working in the technical industry'. Every podcast, every school talk, every university presentation, every article, every career's advert that portrays women in the space allow for role modelling to set in and start making this change happen. Rahma Javed, Director of Engineering at Deliveroo spoke about the significance of raising the industry's profile and more importantly the people within it. She believes, we need to ask ourselves the question 'how many women do we support and promote to the top?' Who are they? And what are their stories? She continued by saying, 'we all want role models! Who are the stories we get inspired by? Your Zuckerbergs, Jobs and Gates and none of them sadly are different from a white male profile but you need to see women at the top and ones that don't just have a career but other responsibilities also'. Rahma called out the need for awareness and all of us to see it as our responsibility to make our next generation more aware of our industry and the abundance of women within it making huge successes.

Kelly Read-Parish, the Chief Operating Officer of Credit Kudos spoke of her personal experience, 'It's incredibly hard to imagine yourself doing something that you have never seen before so for example back in the day it would have been very difficult for a young girl to imagine herself being prime minister if there had never been a female prime minister before'. Translating that to the workplace, she thinks it's really important for both potential and existing employees to see women and people with diverse backgrounds in leadership roles and the qualities of a good leader can be exhibited by anyone, regardless of gender or cultural background. Again, another advocate for everyone having the potential to role model and take it upon themselves to inspire future technology talent. Kimberley Lewis, previous Director at Hermes Investment Management spoke about everyone becoming a mentor to ensure we retain this talent by 'bear hugging' new diverse members of our community. They are 'the ones that are more likely to need more cultivating, they won't have daddy's friend or someone from the golf club to help'. She highlighted that new talent in the industry will need daily support, they will face challenges and there are the 'notorious risk factors' previously stressed so each of us need to be ready to support.

The key here is that we all have a responsibility to affect this and each of us should be asking ourselves what more can I do? and go ahead and do it. The time for pondering is over.

Since the mid-2010s there has been a focus within the community on ensuring that businesses are making their workplaces, 'great places to work' and numerous awards have been garnered in the celebration of that. Many businesses and their leaders have realised that they have to conform to workplace equality if they want to attract new people and grow their company. This has culminated in a number of ways from flexi time, to working from home, better career progression, more open debate, investment in people's skills, and fairer ways of identifying who should be promoted or given a pay rise. The question is now being asked by leaders across the space, 'what do we need to do to be a more attractive workplace?' and in turn a more 'attractive industry?' Many FinTech firms are understanding that challenge, open thought, debate, and collaboration are themes that drive what their staff enjoy at work. It is widely acknowledged that enjoyment sparks employee engagement and that engagement is at the root of productivity.

The statistics as of 2021 show that girls being interested in technology at school level is not improving, however we are becoming more aware of the sheer volume of people within the industry who didn't necessarily study STEM and we are getting better at cross training people into the space. An example of further tackling this comes from Louisa O'Shea, the Chief Executive Officer of Confused.com who felt that rather than just talking about the lack of women coming through from STEM subjects she would support the not-for-profit organisation, FinTech Wales. 'I can influence many more business to help them empower their future leaders whether that be male, female, non-binary and also to create more opportunities for their future leaders and that's something extra to give back'.

Louise is not alone in the 'giving back' and we have seen steps being taken to alter the general perception and reality of the FinTech and Financial Services space through action. Expectations within businesses are being reset, interviews are being improved, onboarding practices are changing, and promotion committees are being implemented to ensure quieter staff or those less likely to ask are not overlooked. There is still much work to be done and I cannot disregard the wider perception problem we all face in the societal barriers regarding women's capabilities, women in leadership, working mothers, and gendered stereotypes. This is where FinTech has a huge potential in breaking down these barriers and debunking these age-old myths that propagate the gendered struggle for parity.

A prominent leader in the Investment Banking space was very vocal about the societal perceptions of gender in the workplace. She opened up by saying 'women can be judged very harshly' at work and not in line with their male counterparts. She implored that we should all be constantly checking ourselves for our own bias. This bias is seen in hiring, in career building, in promotions, in recognition, all subjects we have covered in depth. She called out that she had witnessed women having to be better than the men around them to achieve equal standing. Many others agreed and drew attention to what we then expect of our leaders often putting women into stereotypical 'female' roles or reacting negatively to firm female managers. This particular leader also outlined that looking at hiring, often the one female applicant needs to be by far and above better than 'other twenty male applicants being presented to be considered'. Going further she drew upon more of the realities of hiring in any workplace. She described how every vacancy will need to be signed off and if the hire isn't made quick enough the manager then loses their 'headcount' leaving them no choice but 'to hire under pressure and more likely fall into the trap of hiring another man, often from the same background they always have done'. This takes me back to my initial point where I raised the imperative need for heads of businesses to make the connection between inclusion and their success. only then will they be able to decide whether any of this matters. If long-term business success does matter, then leaders should be considering whether they should invest in educating their staff and implementing that education to end the imbalance in gendered perceptions in the workplace. Furthermore, they should be calling people out on it and halt their progression should they act upon their own prejudices and equally look to re-address their promotion criteria to make it more equal and then identify who has been overlooked in their workplaces.

It was Dagmara of Zumo, who took this concept to the leadership table saying, 'work is needed around the perception of what makes an effective leader - the reality is not what we stereotypically think!' She wanted as much exposure as possible for leaders espousing empathy and collaboration and being wholly committed to making change happen by shining a light on those who are the change. She is fiercely challenging the traditional perception that female leaders can't be firm or direct by being authentic in her methods and being the example, she wishes to set.

The key to Dagmara's message can be found in one of her purest statements, 'when we can truly be ourselves, we can simply perform better'. The clarity for me in this quote draws me to the all-important topic I have only touched upon so far, that of building psychological safety at work. Without this we have no foundations upon which to begin any journey of inclusion.

When I raised all the great steps the industry has made, I also noted that a number of these failed to reach a tipping point because of certain barriers. Psychological safety in the workplace dispels a lot of these barriers. When there is safety, people feel free to talk and more importantly listen, then crucially act upon the newly found knowledge. Fear of change is reduced, and people become more excited about the possibility of new methods and innovation is allowed to flourish. With psychological safety comes discussion rather than the surveys that go unanswered. Surveys have become a commonplace in the financial services and FinTech space as a way for business leaders to identify where their problems lie and what they should know about their team's wishes for the workplace. More often than not the surveys are distributed as anonymous to encourage open feedback. Without psychological safety in the workplace no one has been answering these surveys honestly or openly and sometimes not at all. The newly founded 'Diversity and Inclusion Committees' first task, in my opinion, has been to rectify this through 'listening and acting'. It has been wonderful to see mentoring programmes, buddy systems, open door time allocated in the week, and feedback groups created to allow for a number of different ways for staff to communicate their suggestions or concerns. This type of opinion gathering should be brought into reviews as well and managers who are then targeted on their ability to have open conversation with their team are starting to have more of an impact. The implementation of confidential 'Bias Champions' has made huge progress on how bias is acknowledged and dealt with in a business to ensure it is reduced and expelled altogether. We know that bias still remains commonplace and is often mishandled. Having a person who is qualified to take on confidential information and someone who is trusted in the business to act upon the feedback makes colossal steps forward in this quest. It is important to note two things when we consider how to handle bias effectively. Firstly, we must acknowledge that historically any reporting of bias was met with rebuttals or excuse making and secondly, we can no longer expect the victims of bias to be the ones to report it. We need witnesses speaking up. As previously highlighted, whenever any sort of bias has taken place, there has been a habitual response from management that dismisses this situation, victim blames, excuses the culprit, or gaslights the individual into thinking they have 'got the wrong end of the stick'. When this happens, nothing is done to accept the wrongdoing, reprimand the perpetrator, or educate them and instead their behaviour as a by-product is automatically condoned. In these environments no number of surveys or open forums will work which is why I call for the need to 'listen and act accordingly' instead of 'listen and rebut'. When thinking about the action I call for, I am reminded of Nicola Breyer, the Chief Commercial Officer of OptioPay, and her commitment to learning from her team, through their experiences and their perspectives. She is absolutely devoted to building environments where psychological safety isn't just spoken about but is a reality. She says 'I learn every day and if you are in a learning mindset and in a field, that's developing and moving forward then you will see that not as a role and position and a job title but really how you develop as a person and what you can learn from everything you can do'. She continued to explain how you can learn from everyone you work with if only you give them the freedom to teach you, making every business better and more successful on the journey. For Nicola, it is the constant evidencing to the team that opinions matter, and voices are heard and acted upon. She celebrates people in her business who come up with new ideas, and when sharing those ideas in a wider context will attribute the suggestion to the right person. Action over talking is a significant element of who she is and how she creates this culture. Nicky Koopman, the Senior Vice President of Partnerships for AEVI believes in action too. AEVI is a business that is simplifying face-to-face payments for merchants worldwide making payments technology more accessible to all and therefore incredibly driven by difference of perspective. Nicky felt that if you want people to share their experience with you, you must make it easy to do so and act upon it. As an advocate for authenticity, she said 'diversity and inclusion is not just a phrase, it should be in the DNA of a company.' She went on to give an easy example to implement, imploring people to, 'be alert and actively helping to drive inclusion, if you sit at a table or meeting often the loudest is heard then it's your job to get others to speak'. More action drives the trust building in businesses so that staff trust that they can be themselves and contribute.

Jenny Sadler the Diversity and Talent Acquisition Specialist at MarketAxess, a proprietary trading firm, is leading the charge on this topic. She argues that it's not just about saying 'bring your true self to work' but showing that that will be accepted and furthermore celebrated. An example of this celebration can be seen in how 'difference' is shared through weekly slack calls to build confidence and encourage free flowing ideas. As a team they celebrate culture, festivals, traditions, and much more which builds a safety of what 'makes you unique through positive reinforcement'.

This trust building within businesses is happening often through responding correctly to bias, conscious or unconscious alongside these ways of safety scaffolding. With this multiple feedback forum model, we are starting to see and hear the truth of what is needed to genuinely create environments where people feel included and able to truly prosper. It is imperative that people see the action taken and change implemented to keep this dialogue open. For years the immediate response to any bias reported was that of a rebuttal. We must firstly acknowledge this and then re-educate those who made the excuses as well as reset expectations of those who are expected to raise their hand and share the information. For this to flourish Sophie Guibaud, the Chief Growth Officer of OpenPayd, said it simply needs for 'managers to walk their own talk and then HR can put in processes.' It is then down to everyone else to be vigilant in turning those policies into practice and procedure. Lucy Heavens, the Marketing Director of Wealth Dynamix, raised the point that we still have a long way to go on this topic and therefore a huge opportunity to improve our industry 'there are still people who don't feel comfortable to be themselves and it's everyone's responsibility to create this new normal'.

When I say inclusion is about including everybody it is absolutely essential that we are able to tap into the psyche of everyone in the team to ensure they are working actively to promote inclusion and drive forward initiatives. A large part of this is what I spoke of earlier in the importance of connecting inclusion with success and that resolve coming from the top of organisations and then infiltrating the awareness and action of those below. It was Chirine BenZaied-Bourgerie, the Head of Innovation at Finastra, who made me think of the need for advocates when she said 'gender equality isn't just a women's problem, it's important to have male leaders to talk about the topics to drive more inclusion'. Men who understand why it is important, understand the benefits to the business, to themselves, to society, and are able to explain that to others. With women often still in the minority, having someone in the majority campaign for equity is incredibly powerful and, as Chirine pointed out, very effective at reaching people who may have felt previously that it simply wasn't their battle to fight.

This concept of 'allyship' is crucial to the success of equality in the workplace and raises awareness that quality in the workplace isn't a woman-only issue, it's an everybody issue. The most successful companies are the ones where the advocates are both men and women. It's a responsibility of us all to work with our peers to get it right. Julie Ashmore of NatWest's FinTech, Rapid Cash, agrees and outlines how we can take women-only networking groups a step further to drive faster change. She wholeheartedly believes that 'gender diversity isn't a women's only issue', and said 'I would always caution businesses and teams about creating women's networks as it suggests it's about fixing the women'. Coincidentally when I raised the point of confidence gaps, I noted that the void wasn't in the female ability but instead how that was perceived by the majority around her. When discussing the evidence of women being mentored and upskilled, the barrier wasn't the female skill or potential but instead how that was valued. Therefore, when Julie said 'when we accept that diversity is a business issue then we start to think of better ways to address the issues we face rather than thinking a women's network fixes it.' I was so enamoured by this that I began thinking of what more I could do to connect with the male allies to rally the support needed to drive real actionable change.

If we wish to rally the allies, we have to ensure that everyone feels they can make a difference, that their voice will be heard and that as we previously discussed they are in an environment of psychological safety. There have been multiple calls for action on this topic and many stem from having a psychologically safe environment where everyone feels they can speak up. Laura Rofe the Strategic Partnerships Manager at PPRO demanded that 'education and support is needed from male counterparts for sustainable change'. Lindsey Jayne, the VP of Product for Yoco said 'the most powerful thing is allyship and that means doing what it takes to educate yourself and speak up for others'. When I think about 'speaking up' I am reminded of the number of people who have shared experiences of bias or discrimination and how few were able to cite an advocate who supported them. It is incredibly important to note that in every instance where the person was shielded by an ally they remembered the exact scenario and the empowerment it gave them afterwards to progress and advocate for others. Businesses who are beginning to implement 'Bias Champions', are reaching new levels of movement as people who are witnessing barriers to change now feel they can report bias to a trusted advisor who can affect progression and are trained to handle previously overlooked bias within the business. Appointing a person in this position is happening time and time again across the industry. Those who are already reporting success have the key elements right, a person who is qualified to understand and not deny the issue, trusted to take on the information in safety and in a position of power that they can do the necessary follow-up to prevent similar occurrences. The way this person is endorsed internally is most successful when they are there to react to everyone's opinion and not solely for the victim of bias conscious or unconscious to go to.

Allyship goes beyond standing up for injustices witnessed, and as Arshi Singh the Head of Product at Comply Advantage correctly points out, it is about living and breathing the inclusion by 'walking the talk'. Moreover, it can be taking the first step and in doing so giving permission for others to follow. This is especially important when considering a management-led approach to change. Comply Advantage provides anti-money laundering technology. Founded in 2014 they have built an environment that works proactively for inclusion. As a mother, Arshi was able to tell me about her freedom to speak about her family commitments at work because of how many of the 'men who are now sharing their childcare responsibilities with pride'. Alison Harwood, the Head of London Branch for Varengold Bank said similar, 'for women to be able to reach true equality the focus needs to be on men and how do men feel more supported to take time out if they have children, to be more involved in the home life and being in a position where they are far more empathetic to the challenges women commonly face'. Varengold is a German bank founded in 1995, that partners with FinTechs and specialises in supporting the marketplace lending industry. Alison is a qualified solicitor who now is a qualified finance professional who was nominated for the Women in Credit Rising Star award for 2020 and was a FinTech50 panellist. She runs the UK team and believes much can be done if we affect diversity at the grassroots level, and build equality in every aspect of the job and how the workplace can better support people's personal lives.

Allyship isn't one task, instead it is every part of truly understanding the importance of the mission and wanting to be aware and be part of every element of it. This can be seen in calling out unchallenged bias, in encouraging others to speak out, to correctly attributing praise, to putting forward the correct names for promotion, to onboarding people with potential from places you wouldn't have normally considered, to being open about parental responsibilities and much more. The great news is we are seeing more and more of this especially through the pandemic years.

When considering the maternity experience it has become too copiously clear to me that we must consider the parental experience and share the load both inside and outside of the workplace. We know that working parents have inadequate government support and we know that in society many imbalances remain. However, there is still much that can be done from a workplace perspective that can pave the way for change that will allow for more diversity, more inclusion, and in turn stronger businesses. Much work must be done on supporting the FinTech parental experience should we wish to include FinTech parents in our journey of growth. This isn't just in paid leave or flexible hours upon their return, which I would expect as a minimum but also in understanding the experience, having a culture that supports it, and ensuring that people are genuinely welcomed back. During my first pregnancy in 2019/2020 I recorded a podcast series within a number of men and women across the FinTech and financial services space to help me understand the journey I was embarking on and in particular to help me with my own concerns about my career once a mother. I found that there was little information anywhere about the maternity experience from a career point of view and so I sought solace through building my own podcast series to address it; 'the Maternity and Paternity stories of FinTech'. Every single person I interviewed on that series spoke without exception about the need to 'level up' parental leave and share the responsibility across both parents.

Karen Rudich the Chief Executive Officer of ElementaryB began by saying maternity leave is 'something the financial services industry has made no secret of struggling with'. She cited a number of examples of losing women from the industry because they have to 'make the financial choice of hiring a nanny to raise your child, or not getting paid and not going back to working?'

Crucially, when speaking of the 'juggling act' she was quick to say, 'it's also a juggling act for men and organisations forget about the fact that men also want to be there; they also want to go to the school play, yet they also want to have the career'. We discussed at length the possibility of having both, the family and the career and what workplaces should be doing to support both parents to allow for them to participate in both sides of their lives. This was largely variations of shared parental leave, open conversation around what the incumbent wants for their career and family and the flexibility of hours. Getting this right Karen explained will 'propel businesses forward' if they encourage and support when returning parents to the workforce, they 'will benefit from their talent and delivery'.

Alex Ford, the VP of Product and Marketing at Encompass Corporation, equally raised the affordability choice many women have to make. Based in Australia, Alex said, that they face similar childcare affordability challenges to those we see here in the UK and alongside the gender pay gap 'returning to work doesn't make a financial sense' for some mothers. In addressing the solution similarly to Karen, she felt that men should have the 'same opportunities to be involved in parenting, when that happens it allows women to readjust the balance'.

Diana Paredes, the Chief Executive Officer and Co-Founder of Suade Labs is incredibly active on this subject and argues that 'affordable/subsidised childcare should be a right not a privilege'. Taking it beyond what we can do as a FinTech and financial services community ourselves internally, Diana is a huge advocate for working to do more externally. She said, 'statutory leave for men is two weeks and there is no support from the government, so the FinTech community should be demanding more from the government'. Diana's business is revolutionising the way financial institutions comply with regulation. She is all about policies that should be in place to protect people and allow for continued success. Just as managers of businesses need to connect success with inclusion so does our government in their assigning of policy and support. Looking back to what is in our power right now to affect Gabriel MacSweeney, Strategic Partnerships and Commercial Strategy at Codat, said that in addressing this balance 'shared parental leave is an absolute must within any business' and will fast track gender equality. Elena Betes Novas, the Chief Executive Officer of RVU, the business that owns Confused.com, said that for real change to take place there must be 'equal terms for maternity and paternity leaves as it changes dynamics in hiring and it puts every candidate on the same frame'.

This again has been a sentiment supported by huge numbers in the community. However very few businesses implement it at the moment.

Leaders often feel that they will be giving time or money away and miss the connection they make to gaining loyal, committed members of staff because their family needs have been considered. Let us not forget the huge opportunity the FinTech community faces in its growth and the need for an engaged workforce. Celine Crawford, the Chief Communications Officer of Smarkets spoke about the realities of parental support and its link to people's loyalty. 'You want a really positive ecosystem for people to flourish whether they are parents or not.' This directly correlates to business objectives as you need the staff to be able to drive those objectives forward. She celebrated Smarkets' policies that support a lengthy maternity policy, emergency nannying, and even having a parent's room where children in the workplace are welcomed. This ongoing support of parental responsibility is hugely important. It's not just within the policy but the taking up of the policy that matters. Several women I interviewed reminded me 'you would be surprised at how few parents take shared parental leave if they can'. They spoke of the realities within company culture, especially those where the management don't openly support and live by the policies themselves. Each of them opened my eyes to the significance of senior members of staff taking up these policies once they are in place, to show by example they are truly embraced. Only then will this change mindsets and get men more involved and allow for women to return from maternity and feel that they are welcomed back. Ben Wulwik, Head of Legal and Transaction Execution at OakNorth Bank, supported this argument telling me of what he had witnessed in other businesses. He felt that shared parental leave wasn't as much about giving the option, but actually in the take up on it because of the lack of acceptance within company culture and societal culture. He went on to explain that when shared parental leave was first implemented in a business he knew of, 'at the start questions were asked "is this guy serious about his career?" Now a few years later it's totally accepted'. Ben felt the real question was in 'how do you prevent that first one or two with that stigma? It absolutely comes from the top, with a message "this is what we are offering there is no stigma around" and that the business supports it'. Another example of how new policies are simply not enough, we need to think about environment and safety to reach our tipping point.

Part of my 'Maternity and Paternity stories of FinTech' was about speaking to the community to help new mothers and fathers feel more welcomed back to work and to instil confidence in those around me that there are people who desperately want to return to work just in a way that they can and is made possible for them. In speaking to men and confirmed 'allies' I found myself feeling encouraged about the potential of how far this industry can drive forward equality through the parental journey.

In talks with David Brear, the Chief Executive Officer of 11:FS, it was really refreshing to hear about his thoughts on the practicalities of what maternity and paternity entails with regard to returning to work. In his opening statement on the subject, he was quick to say 'start-up founders can make dumb decisions on that (maternity leave) but equally I have seen big corporates use maternity leave as an opportunity to reshuffle and it's not fair and doesn't treat people as individuals' and in fact it's a sure fire way to lose staff quickly. He went on to connect the success of 11:FS and their fast, sustainable growth due to the way each person has been treated, as individuals whose personal lives matter, whose opinions are counted for, and whose passions allow the business to thrive. He went on to talk about building the business and how 'we over index on people who are passionate about what they do whether they are a product manager or engineer so we see confident in the fact that they love the thing that they are doing,' meaning that when they do take time to have a child it's not about losing all connection if they don't want it to be. Instead he works hard to keep engagement up depending on what that person wants. I was in my second trimester of my first pregnancy when we recorded this podcast, and it gave me so much confidence that I could return to work after maternity and that actually I could do a bit of work during my maternity so not to lose touch with the business. This is exactly what I did do and really helped me with my birth recovery and happiness levels post birth.

Ben Wulwik, of OakNorth Bank raised another pertinent issue, namely that of investigating what a person wants from their career when they begin or grow their family. He said, 'generally businesses don't ask the questions, they don't appreciate what the working side of the parental relationship goes through, there is a general appreciation that you just cope and that's not the case for everyone'. His call to action was to remember the human involved, that predominantly the financial support is what is spoken about over the personal well-being. He implored that companies have a duty of care to help and more critically understand what each person's aspirations are over this period and that 'everyone is different and will need different levels of support. Someone may want the promotion and others will want to be more flexible and be at home more'. Ben spoke about being a father and knowing that many dads want to take their children to nursery, but without the well-being conversations happening as early as they should or as regularly as they should, 'often fathers are overlooked altogether'. To achieve parity in the workplace including men in the conversation of childcare and parental leave is imperative.

Kelly Read-Parish, Chief Operating Officer of Credit Kudos, who recently went on maternity leave following the birth of her daughter, has helped shape and promote company policy around both maternity and Shared Parental Leave. Kelly explained 'I personally thought it was very important to encourage my husband to take an equivalently long Shared Parental Leave (as my maternity leave), both to spend time with our new baby and also to help normalise men taking advantage of family policies'. She continued, 'until men see other men taking advantage of schemes like Shared Parental Leave, we will continue to see slow uptake and a higher penalty for women who take maternity leave'.

Diana Paredes felt that without well-being conversations, we make it more difficult for parents to make any return to work happen. 'You would be surprised how many women want to get back to work but there isn't the option for a lot of them'. Agreeing with Ben she went on to say how everyone wants something different or have different needs. In her personal situation she wanted her baby to be physically close to her upon swift return to the office. Indeed, Diana returned to work very quickly and brought her baby to the office with the nanny so that she was 'physically close'. This led her to discuss options for childcare, such as government subsidised creches on site or close to the City of London and concluded that 'If we want women to work, we need to give them the option to come back to work'. Giving the option to come back isn't just about a job offer. Instead, it is key to discuss the parameters in which someone returns and, whether a mother or father, their aspirations and abilities are considered alongside those of the business. Sometimes the solution is about creating an environment where flexible hours are linked to productivity. Other options are about having the open culture where everyone feels they can be a co-worker and a mum or dad. Further solutions have been found in job shares so that those who need more time to care for family can do so whilst adding value to the business. Diana also pointed out that she only 'realised how little awareness I had around the topic of maternity and paternity until I had a child' and now she feels compelled to bring everyone on the journey in their own way. This awareness is an incredible driver for me personally and reflects what I am trying to do with this book. In talks with Diana, we spoke about how unappealing balancing a baby and a career at the same time is traditionally described in this sector, especially when you want both. We wanted to affect change by sharing our stories and those of others too to openly highlight the challenges but more important show its possibility. This is particularly important for where it has been achievable and more significantly where it has been successful. Too many people feel they have to miss out on parenthood, others question if they will have to sacrifice their career and worse still many have felt they don't have a choice to make it work. I am a passionate advocate for creating the compromise for us all so that no one needs the work or family ultimatum.

Elena Betes Novas is walking the talk on this and told me of how she's hired two Chief Executive Officers when they were pregnant. Patricia Salume spoke about receiving funding for VeeLoop when she was heavily pregnant describing it as 'very refreshing that there are some people out there that can see beyond'. She put this down to her having a clear plan and being able to talk her investors through that plan because they wanted to hear it.

These are examples of how knowing each and everyone's unique perspective and situation is key to the success of making a career and family work. This knowledge needs to be acted upon correctly. I loved how Nicola Dennes, the Global Talent Acquisition Lead at Marex called for more of this saying 'if someone said they were going to do an MBA you would sit down with them and ask what your time commitment is here? What sort of financial support are you after? It's a clear and unique conversation but when talking about pregnancy people lack the confidence'. Nicola went on to remind us of the importance of empowering and training members of the management team to be able to have 'confident conversations around the individual because every pregnancy is different'.

The majority of what I am raising in this chapter is about changing our thinking and challenging the way things are currently done. Just as I highlighted in the previous chapters, lots of good work is happening but to reach the tipping point, we need to take that good work a bit further often by breaking down the obstacles in the way through tackling foundations of the businesses who wish to drive this change. The maternity conversation is not just about pay and when you return but exactly how you want that to be and what the fathers want and how we build an environment where everyone is welcomed back because everyone was able to make it the experience they wanted regardless of gender.

Similarly, when we reflect on how new members of staff are recruited, we must question the entire system and consider whether it is driving the results we seek. For thirty years, the way we recruit people to the financial services, technology and now FinTech sector has largely remained the same. The methods of applicant attraction may have evolved, most notably the use of social media platforms and email marketing, however the way in which businesses reach out to advertise they are looking has stayed static. Typically, any firm looking to grow will decide what person they need and write up a description of that person's skill set in a tick list format and advertise that hire. The methods of how these requirements are advertised used to be written adverts in newspapers, then on the internet via search engines and now on various media platforms that allow for a wider audience to see the opportunities available. Having started my recruitment career in 2005, recruiting technologists into the financial services sector largely revolved around learning what the hiring manager wanted in 'his' team and attracting people to that role with as close to the capability the manager had described. The managers were all men, bar a handful and the people they hired were hired specifically to be 'culturally similar' so they would 'fit in'. There was no talk of growth mindset, challenging the status quo and definitely no diversity of thought. Attracting the candidates consisted of using a database which you populated daily with new contacts, writing adverts to be posted on three 'job boards' and headhunting which was done by telephone networking through businesses you learnt about from your contacts. 17 years on, the attraction process has had a shift to the online and the automated. Adverts still exist, headhunting is often through mediums such as Linked In and outbound email marketing and social selling via a variety of online platforms has risen exponentially to allow for better networking, event-led relationship building, a faster outreach process, and a wider range. To fulfil vacancy requirements recruiters have had to become far more proactive in their candidate attraction methodologies to allow them to be able to have the networks of applicants to share with hiring managers as they request their vacancies filled. The problem we still face is that women are underrepresented in this process despite the steps forward many businesses have made, including addressing gendered language in adverts and introducing quota systems. The one thing that hasn't changed at all is the system in place where a hiring manager's request for a new hire is when they need that new hire. Furthermore, at that point in time that new hire is identified with a list of skills that person must have. Herein lies the biggest opportunity for us all.

Lauren McEwan the Records Manager at the Pension Protection Fund said that for the sector to grow a more gender-balanced workforce we need to take the change much further and 'we need to shake up how we hire technologists'. It was then, Seema Khinda Johnson, Co-Founder of Nuggets who said, 'when growing or scaling your business you can't be reactive only if you want to build diverse teams'. I have always believed that working as a recruiter has never been about finding someone their next job and walking away, but instead helping people build their careers and helping businesses grow and scale their mission. I quickly became acutely aware of the responsibility I had to improve this industry through how it attracts people, retains people, and invests in those people to make everyone more engaged in their workplaces and therefore make those workplaces that much more successful.

Rather than waiting for someone to 'shake up' how we 'proactively' recruit I started thinking what I could do to affect the gender imbalance across the sector in general from junior to mid-level to senior and C Level.

For a number of years, I have been sharing my 'Talent Triangle Theorem' as a proactive solution to hiring for potential and people growth. My Theorem isn't necessarily gender focused but solves the problem of hiring people for what they know now, over what they can learn and, more importantly, what potential they have. Often people in hiring positions are under time constraints to hire as their vacancy arise, due to a need identified in their department to replace a lost incumbent or to grow for a specific project, it's all too easy to commoditise applicants by seeking the 'finished article' or 'someone who can hit the ground running'. This type of hiring does not accommodate the applicants wants, needs, career, or progression and must be addressed. When firms identify their gender gaps, frequently I see them starting their hiring process without considering the applicant's potential or career journey. The 'Talent Triangle Theorem' has been my way of exhibiting how we hire in a three pronged manner by investing in people, growing their careers, and helping them learn new skills. Instead of hiring for someone with skill set ABCD because you want that skill set now you should look at the pool of people who have skills ABC for example and pledge to teach then D or E or F. Simple? Yes, effective? yes when used, popular? Not as much as it should be since human beings are still tied to doing things the way they have always done unless there is enough of a pull to make change happen. This is the reason for me saying we must affect the foundations first, have the leaders drive this, and not allow for procrastination. We have a duty to build our next generation of managers, leaders, and board members. It is up to us who we should do that with and my call to action is largely around doing it ourselves rather than waiting for the mythical 'someone else' to solve it.

The podcast series taught me to take this further. In 2019, Helen Smith, the Chief Operating Officer of Cashflows calls upon on the recruitment industry saying, 'I would like to see executive head-hunters and recruiters take more of a firmer position on this, challenging Chief Executive Officers and Chairs to genuinely open their minds from Board rooms to executives with different backgrounds, experiences and allegiances'. She went on to explain that when trying to affect the gender balance 'at the top' of organisations often, 'the HR function plays a supportive role in the recruitment of C suite and Boards, so recruiters should look to step in as a true business partner to advise and challenge established ways of thinking'. As such recruiters and head-hunters 'have a big responsibility' to find people from different places and break the cycle of recruiting people who talk and think the same.

It was Iraide Ruiz and Ridhima Durham, who in sharing their experience, drove me to turn an idea into a campaign to further drive change. Iraide Ruiz, the Technology Manager and Technology Diversity Champion at IG, told me of how she was hired there. She was speaking at an event held at the IG offices on the topic of 'imposter syndrome' and following the talk was approached by a senior manager asking her if he could build a role for her there. Similarly, Ridhima Durham, the Chief Commercial Officer of Salary Finance, an employee benefits platform shared how she had progressed within her career. She explained how she had got a lot of her roles through her networks and in fact 'I had roles created for me at both Wonga and Bond Street. They were looking for talented individuals, they were looking for something specific and I didn't quite fit in, so they created something new for me'. She went on to share that throughout her career she has been offered high-profile roles that she turned down because they lacked flexibility and creativity. She implored the listeners to 'look for that talented individual and think about how you create something for them, be willing to tap into your networks and your network's network and think about people who don't fit your typical profile' concluding that 'you might be pleasantly surprised'.

By the time I had recorded my 150th episode of the 'Women of FinTech' podcast series, 97 of those interviewed had had a role created for that at some point in their career and I decided launching my '17% List' campaign was the right thing to have done as it had quite enough evidence. During the summer of 2020 I spent a lot of time with my new-born baby girl walking around the City of London, a City deserted due to the lockdown and pandemic. I thought a lot about what the continuing gender imbalance within the Financial Services and FinTech community would mean for my little girl should she wish to join the sector in 18 years' time. It was then that gravity of the figure 17% hit me. Not only at the time did we only have 17% of all technology positions in the UK filled by women but worse still, as I have raised numerous times before, this figure has been the same for a number of years. I felt something had to be done. With my vast recruitment experience I knew the concept of 'role creations' was key, more importantly I knew I had to help hiring managers see the women they often didn't believe existed in developer, architecture, DevOps, Cyber Security, or project manager roles. A common phrase cited in recruitment conversations is that 'women don't exist in this particular space' and I wanted to dispel this myth. I want to stop people accepting this as a reason we are not improving the statistics and ask the real questions as to why. 17% needs to grow and it is low but it's not 1%. There are areas more challenging than others however my campaign was to draw awareness to whom did exist and give them more opportunities.

Within 6 months of launching my campaign I have had 140 FinTech and financial services organisations subscribe to my list and every two weeks they receive communication from me sharing evidence upon evidence that women do exist in technology roles. Within the first 6 months over 100 vacancies specific to this campaign were unearthed and a third of these were totally new roles created specifically for the women I shared. Please note these first 6 months were during the 2020 and 2021 pandemic. The premise of the campaign is to turn recruitment upside down and, as Seema had demanded, make recruitment more 'proactive'. I openly highlight that this alone won't solve the problem but in conjunction with the other elements within these pages it does allow for actionable transformation within the sector.

The investment into people and their progression, is intimately linked to succession planning, should we see any success. Having spoken at length about the learning mindset, agility, and resilience found in so many FinTech and financial services cultures, there is so much opportunity for us to lead the charge and really affect the numbers we see. 17% is a dismal figure and one we can commit to affect should we ensure we not only attract a better gender balance to the industry but retain them and build upon their skills. I love seeing this in action and watching how people grow their careers through businesses when they are given the opportunity. A brilliant example of this came from Amrita Srivastava, Head of FinTechs for Mastercard, Western Europe. She is a big believer in encouraging people from varied experiences to grow in the industry so much so that she tells us about how her own journey into the world of tech where she was hired for '50% for what I know (finance) and 50% for what I can learn (technology)'. Amrita is an advocate for encouraging others from diverse backgrounds to enter tech and to hire and build their teams with this philosophy.

Iraide Ruiz felt that the solution largely lay in this opportunity too and explained one of IG's initiative to build a more gender-balanced team. The example she cited was a technology onboarding programme which allowed the team 'to train someone who has been transferred from another department'. She continued that they were launching this 'externally to allow candidates to learn with us and have their first role in technology within our group'. I am a big fan of this type of thinking and am often reminded of the UK education sector and their work in attracting people with management experience to retrain as teachers on a fast track programme, often within an 18-month period, and then move into Deputy head positions in our school system. Thinking about options for the financial services and FinTech community I like to use the term 'triple jumping' where I encourage businesses to affect their gender imbalance by identifying management or leadership skills from outside the industry and 'hop, skip and jump' them into technology, into finance and back up into leadership on an accelerated learning programme similar to what has worked well in the education sector. Dr Louise Ryan of Close Brothers demands that more should be done across the whole industry to 'cross train our current staff', then 'promote those who are successful' and ultimately 'retain and nurture good female talent'. Seeing a number of women across FinTech and financial services businesses in roles outside of technology, she feels passionately about giving them the opportunity to learn and progress within the sector.

Professor Sue Black OBE is literally walking the talk on this concept having founded BCSWomen, the UK's first online network for women in tech, and #techmums, a social enterprise which empowers mums and their families through technology. She does all this alongside her work as a Professor of Computer Science at Durham University. She says, 'having been in technology for 25 years now I've quite often heard that companies want to hire more women into technology roles, but they can't find them, or they don't apply, or they do apply and don't make it through the interview process and at the same time across those 25 years I've met so many women with so much potential who want to work in technology but don't quite know how to get there'. It is no wonder Professor Sue was named one of Forbes World #Top50 Women in Technology as she has been an inspiring champion for women in technology and used £1 million funding from the Institute of Coding for her groundbreaking TechUPWomen project where in its first year she took 100 women from the Midlands and North from underrepresented backgrounds into technology careers. Professor Sue sees it very simply, she trains women up to find jobs in the industry saying that there are 'no more excuses to hiring diverse talent'. Succession planning is then about taking this potential and investing in it. Having spoken at length about the 'overlooked' or those who haven't been assigned 'credit' for their contribution Mary Agbesanwa's words ring true when she said, 'how do we support people better?' When considering their progression in this sector, 'for many people its countercultural to be self-promoting' and as showcased in many 'organisations self-promotion helps you progress'. Mary Agbesanwa is FinTech Scale Programme Lead at PWC, she co-leads PwC's award-winning Multicultural Business Network, co-runs a millennial women's networking and personal development community called 'Now You're Talking' and she was named as Standout 35 in the 2020 Innovate finance women in FinTech Powerlist. When she spoke about the challenges people have with self-promotion, she was talking from a wider diversity perspective to that only of gender. She works tirelessly to 'educate empower and engage the BAME community' with a view to break down their 'stereotypes of this space'. Through her ever-growing 'Now You're Talking' community she works with women to create a safe space for learning, support, sponsorship, and confidence building to help them on their career journeys. As we spoke, I felt increasingly compelled to address the issue of the 'overlooked' in a way that didn't require them to have to advocate for themselves but for us to create an environment where they can 'bloom'. Addressing this successfully is happening across the FinTech space through what is becoming known as 'promotion boards' or 'promotion committees' where groups of senior staff meet up to discuss one thing only, the potential of those within their business that haven't spoken up or fought for themselves to be seen as the next person to achieve a pay rise or title advancement. Everyone has a responsibility to advocate for others should we wish for this cycle to break.

Breaking the cycle can be found in training and crucially the follow-up and implementation of key learns. Upskilling is a huge part of achieving results but needs to be implemented and more importantly followed up in a way that is authentic and led from the top because the connection between success and inclusion has been made. Training as highlighted previously can and should cover a plethora of subjects outside the popular 'unconscious bias awareness' to include psychological safety, speaking about race, handling bias appropriately, promoting those who don't advocate for themselves, encouraging opinion sharing, knowing how to motivate a diverse team, having open and planned parental leave conversations, and so on. The follow-up to training that has proved successful has been seen in the swelling numbers of audits and measurability implemented within businesses to ensure that the lessons are learnt and implemented. This correct follow-up allows for us to close in on our tipping point. It was Elena Betes Novas, the Chief Executive Officer of RVU that said we need to affect middle management and 'force people to think without bias'. Having structures in place to tie management promotions and career progression to the success of their inclusion practices is one way of doing this. Implementing shared parental leave was another suggestion she made for forcing the playing field to be levelled. Arshi Singh the Head of Product at Comply Advantage spoke of how training needs to be around changing perceptions of a leader and what leadership looks like itself, describing how the image many of us that conjure up in our heads of a leader, 'fist thumping the table' isn't necessarily what it takes to be a great leader nowadays. She went on to cite that 'the more senior you are the bigger impact you have on your teams' therefore the responsibility to lead from the front and 'live and breathe' training learns becomes even more important. Training and its follow-up were also discussed in conversation with Michelle

Johnson the Head of UK and Ireland for Fexco Payments and FX. She sees that the success of the unconscious bias training has principally been due to the fact that it was 'top down and our Chief Executive Officer took the first step', allowing for their staff to follow with confidence and trust. Thinking about successful follow-up there have been many examples where the leadership team has been successful because they have been held accountable for results and these results are assessed and measured. Regular audits allow for progress to happen and then be celebrated further cementing the need for safety and inclusion. Katharine Wooller of Daxci spoke fervently about changing the system from the top, in particular reference to growing teams. As a reminder, Daxci are able to boast a gender balance of 55% women and she highlights that 'people tend to recruit in their own image. You don't want 99 clones of the senior management and nearly always they will be white middle class males who will identify with and get on better with and seek to promote broadly other middle class white males'. Breaking this cycle has to be implemented top down and without this top down approach all the hard work training middle managers can be ineffectual. This is similarly true when I raised the points earlier around gendered leadership and what people expect of a leader, with us walking the talk here and women receiving C-level backing change through discussion will be sluggish at best.

Driving change must also include the definitive and bold actions needed to end the gaps that still exist. Notably the gender pay gap is a problem that persists and acts as a huge anchor for progress. This has proved difficult for business leaders who are challenged by current salary discrepancies, prior promotions based on those who demanded it, and of course the big issue of hiring people on a 5 or 10% increase on their current salary. Inadvertently here in the UK many leaders still follow the policy of paying people a percentage increase on their current salary rather than paying them what they deem their potential and skill set it worth. Breaking this standard practice will immediately make an effect. Celine Crawford of Smarkets spoke about how 'we committed to transparent pay a number of years ago, it has its challenges, but we are proud to be working against the gender pay gap'. Making this decision understandable has its complexities and will need to be an all-or-nothing approach however looking at what inclusion can do for valuation, revenue, and profits, this really should be more of a consideration. Closing the pay gap needs measurement, goal setting, and for the leaders to truly believe in the cause. This is a choice for every business, and it is good to see so many more choosing to voluntarily reveal their gender pay gap statistics and pledge to work to improve. With this type of transparency and commitment will drive change but without government enforcement its is still the choice of the few.

Many external events have both hindered and expedited these topics and it's to them I now wish to turn.

10

Help or Hindrance: External Factors

There are several external factors that have affected the financial services and FinTech community in the drive towards a better and more successful workplace. Notably the COVID-19 crisis, the government's input on the gendered struggle, societal changes, investor decision-making, and the rise of a people-first workplace culture has helped or hindered the inclusion mission in different ways. To ensure we can all take part in the change needed, I must be open about these factors.

Looking at the COVID-19 pandemic as a starting point. The whole world was thrown into chaos in early 2020 with the speed at which the deadly coronavirus spread. By March 2020 UK Prime Minister, Boris Johnson, conceded that the UK needed to go into a lockdown to reduce transmission of the disease and prevent the national health service from being totally engulfed by it. Overnight the entire UK FinTech and financial services sector had to transition working from home and colleagues could only work together virtually. Vanessa Vallely OBE, Founder of WeAreTheCity, said of that time 'when COVID-19 first hit it was such a shock to everyone', we asked ourselves 'how do we survive? how do we mobilise an at home workforce overnight?' The reality was that we did. Many industries and their workforces were tragically forced to stop working. The UK government implemented furlough schemes to attempt to keep people financially afloat despite not being able to work and women were hit hardest. We have seen that the worldwide impact of COVID-19 has been catastrophic for so many people with millions affected and millions more lives lost to this terrible disease. Looking at how the

© The Author(s), under exclusive license to Springer Nature Switzerland AG 2022
N. Edwards-Dashti, *FinTech Women Walk the Talk*,
https://doi.org/10.1007/978-3-030-90574-3_10

pandemic has affected people beyond the immediate impact of the disease itself we see through many reports that it has been women who have lost their jobs at a higher rate than men. Women have been furloughed more and with nurseries and schools that had to close in lockdown, many mothers were forced to leave their jobs simply not being able to work and instead take on the majority of the childcare. Sheryl Sandberg, the Chief Operating Officer of Facebook, famously coined the phrase the 'double-double shift' when describing working mothers who were managing to work their full-time jobs, care and educate their children whilst keeping on top of the household duties, let alone those who also cared for other family members. In 2021 the consultancy PWC produced several reports where they depicted the results of the crisis on women in the workplace, their unemployment, job losses, and the result leading to a spiralling of the gender pay gap. They warned that a 'shecession' was inevitable unless gender equality is increased quickly.

With regard to the FinTech and financial services sector we saw a number of businesses fail and collapse, however, it certainly wasn't the majority. Many businesses had to pivot their product offering and did so effectively, responding quickly to demand in an economy that needed ecommerce, global money transfers and online payment transactions to work and work well. Others did have to respond to the crisis by reducing their workforce to stay afloat and there was a particular strain on those who relied on the hospitality sector for their transaction demands. Even so the FinTech and financial services' experience has been largely unlike that of any other sector worldwide because of its ability to move its staff to the virtual. Where other sectors have been ravaged by the disease and the lockdowns, there have been many FinTech firms who have thrived because of their ability to reach a customer base that grew, notably the ecommerce sector.

As such, the FinTech experience has largely been about handling the challenges the pandemic threw up and trying to rise to them to survive and in some circumstances, many have been able to flourish. In talks with Rita Martins, the FinTech Partnerships Lead of Innovation Finance and Risk at the well-known bank HSBC, we discussed the agility the sector had to showcase in their response. A big believer in the power of new ideas and implementing them, Rita said 'everyone was an innovator in lockdown, everyone had to be inventive and look at a problem from a different angle'. The 'FinTech mindset' had to go into overdrive to allow for the business to reposition and remarket themselves in totally new ways. Rebecca Duckworth, Chief Sales and Marketing Officer of QV Systems, was an inspiration when she shared that 'COVID-19 has allowed us to build out new propositions and accelerate strategies in our business'. An example she used was to showcase their steps forward in making their product more digitally friendly to meet the demands of the time.

It was Monika Gupta who really made me think about how inseparable the topic of diversity is to the potential survival of businesses during this crisis. Monika Gupta is the UK Managing Director of a global firm called Decimal Factor, a regulated credit broker. She is ardent about the power of teams thriving when they work well together. Describing the industry as a whole and the businesses she knew who were reacting well to the pandemic she said, 'a mix of genders brings stability and different points of view, it brings emotional intelligence and that's what we needed in business during the pandemic'.

Liza Russell, Chief Operating Officer of Inbotiqa, said the time raised the need for cross-community collaboration and a togetherness we hadn't seen before. Liza explained that her business was 'ahead of the curve as remote working is what we do' and how she felt the need to 'share those ideas across the FinTech community' at a time where it was totally new to most organisations. Businesses partnered and online communities cropped up to discuss a plethora of people-focused topics from; how do you ensure your staff remain engaged when working from home, to how can we best onboard a new member of staff remotely? In the gloom, this is where the light began to shine and leaders recognised the true strength of their companies lay in the people that work there.

Louise O'Shea, the Chief Executive Officer of Confused.com, called out the need for people focused strategies across the whole industry very early on in the pandemic when she described it as a 'very real test of culture'. She went on to elaborate, saying 'we've all had to respond to new ways of working, we've all had personal circumstances that have been highly stressful and none of us could have predicted any of this'. She felt passionately that 'the organisations that have responded well in terms of looking after their employees and responded well in terms of their performance are the ones that have the really strong cultures and have a highly supportive environment'. Louise has built an environment and culture where her people feel safe and supported, she is proud to say that they know 'their interests are at the top of our agenda' and in turn she believes 'they will pay that back tenfold in terms of what they will achieve for Confused.com'.

Vanessa Vallely recalled the sheer volume of 'great stories' she heard across the entire technology sector about how businesses 'kept people engaged and it was more of a case of looking after their teams, making sure that everyone was ok and focusing on the culture of the organisation whilst we all go through this challenging time together'. It was brilliant to see how humanity rose to the surface and how with the workplace becoming people's bedrooms, kitchens and living rooms so did an understanding that staff are mothers, fathers, carers to elderly parents, dog lovers, or horticultural enthusiasts. As we opened up our main window of communication to the video call, we shared our homes and home lives with our colleagues.

Dr Ruth Wandhöfer, partner at the FinTech focused Venture Capital firm Gauss Ventures, felt this new awareness of the workplace and the homelives of one another 'finally it brings everyone on a level playing field'. She went on to say 'whether single, in a partnership or you have children, that equality of everyone being able to work from home' brings a realisation that would have taken years to land otherwise. She also highlighted that this new awareness wasn't confined to the workplace but rather at home where 'families were having to share things between them form child education to home schooling and looking after the household'. This in itself is an incredibly important component for the shared parental leave debate and the perception barriers around it that we seek to break. Again, Rebecca Duckworth gave a brilliant example of how 'COVID-19 has allowed us to learn that some of the people we had part time could really work full time because the flexibility' of not travelling in 'allowed them to have balance and allowed them to take care of their children or parents and has given us the opportunity to look at our workforce moving forward'. It is these such examples that we must share across all workplaces should we want to find some positive in the dreadful times the pandemic threw at us all.

Long before the pandemic had taken hold, I spoke with Annette Evans, the Vice President of People and Culture at Global Processing Systems, in a 'Maternity and Paternity Stories of FinTech' podcast where she spoke about her method of 'smarter working' to get the best out of your people and for them to get the best out of you. I now call her a 'pre-pandemic pioneer' when I remember her words, 'I'm not a big fan of using the phrase flexible working, I like using smarter working' where it 'doesn't have to be bums on seats in the office - it can be anywhere, here at GPS we have a great infrastructure that enables our business continuity plan outside the office'. When we discussed why this method of working was so limited across the sector, she explained that when people ask for flexibility, 'you get a lot of managers that say no that won't work, but then ask yourself the question, are you putting in an imaginary blocker of resistance and for what reason? We sometimes create reasons in our heads when in hindsight it doesn't really make any sense'. Vanessa Vallely also spoke of great cultures and environments best set up for success, saying that COVID-19 had allowed progress for the working from home concept that 'would have taken years and years any other way'. She explained that numerous organisations had spoken to her about their shift away from presenteeism to productivity. Most virtual workers would recall at the time that physical presenteeism was replaced by online presenteeism during the pandemic and with the toll that took on people's welfare and mental health to such an extreme that managers and business leaders had to respond. Vanessa said it became about 'the well-being of our teams' and that for any business to be successful they needed to understand that 'your business is your people, so it's an absolute must to look after them'. Andrea Sparke, Managing Director and Head of Sales EMEA for Toppan Merrill, spoke about how we must eradicate the culture of fear that if you are not in the office, you aren't working hard, by ensuring we are 'giving everyone that power and ability to show they can be productive whilst keeping them connected'. She is an advocate for real psychological safety in the workplace and equated the flexibility and work from home offered to office workers as a huge step forward in attracting new and different types of people to the industry. Alex Ford, the VP of Product and Marketing for Encompass Corporation, agrees, saying that the pandemic and its challenges uprooted several themes, 'there is a welfare angle to this and an equality angle, also there's a really strong economic case' with regard to 'the productivity and returns you get back' by properly supporting your workforce. She spoke of how through absolute 'necessity we have learnt how work can be more accessible' to all whilst implementing 'structural changes which will give us the social and economic returns' in the long run.

Dr Ruth Wandhöfer spoke about his too, believing that 'the current crisis is a great opportunity to attract women to the industry because you can work from home'. Taking it further she felt that in showcasing how the industry is able to survive whilst working virtually, not only will women be drawn to the space but will find it easier to stay and thrive without having to choose between a career and childcare or other family responsibilities saying, 'I really hope this becomes a long-term positive consequence out of this! There are many types of jobs that can be done digitally so this is really the future'. This has been a common thread of the potential the pandemic has shown us all. Ritu Singh the Regional Business Director for StoneX, a broker dealer, powerfully said 'FinTech will allow you to balance your work around your life rather than balance your life around your work' and still be uber successful. This is not the perception of the industry just yet and she works hard to raise awareness of how there is a potential for real flexibility and the learns from the pandemic years has allowed for us all to shift away from presenteeism in the workplace and instead focus on productivity. This exact point was raised by Serena Koivurinta, a Senior Product Portfolio Owner at Caplin, when she shared her story and within it, her years working within consultancies.

Her experience there was that her work was all-consuming and infiltrated her breakfast through meetings and even her gym session. She described her move and attraction to Caplin, a successful web trading technology provider to the global financial markets as one where "I came to the FinTech space for work life balance and more importantly balance in the workplace." Serena is a big believer in the power of balance to allow for better productivity and more efficient ways of working whilst being aware of your needs and mental well-being. These are real examples more people need to know about should we change the perception of the space.

I absolutely acknowledge that there are still many organisations that don't subscribe to an enlightened culture but as Andrea Sparke of Toppan Merrill said in a roundtable with me, 'the pandemic has given the opportunity to reset and recalibrate your culture'. Increasing numbers of firms are making the connection between inclusion and success and are starting to change their ways. Andrea highlights what a brilliant opportunity the discussion around return the office can be for these businesses who want to become more inclusive and attractive to people from different backgrounds to those they have attracted before.

Looking at this on a more macro level, I constantly talk about the power of an engaged, talented, upskilled, invested in, and psychologically safe individual in the workplace, let alone a team, company, and wider industry. When we contemplate the positive impact of building this into the industry we can therefore begin to expect a positive impact on the wider economy. As we talk about the economic recovery post pandemic, we absolutely must consider these themes. Debbie Forster, MBE, of the Tech Talent Charter, inspired me to speak as much as I do about 'retraining' people to allow them a career within the space when she explained, 'lots of people are being displaced from jobs—they are intelligent, talented, enthusiastic people and they can power companies and the economy back'. Specifically speaking about women, Alex Ford believes that 'as we recover from COVID-19 we need to tap into the potential of the entire population, not just half of it'. Her call to action was that for the good of the global economy we need to rally together. As the debates about how workers are returning to their offices and what their cultures will look like rages on, numerous people in the FinTech space warned me about what the 'new normal' may look like. Rita Martins of HSBC was one to identify that whilst many businesses have taken on a people approach and invested into diversity, equity, inclusion, well-being, productivity, and mission-led conversations, many others have allowed for the inclusion conversation to be put on the back burner. They have done this in the guise that the businesses' survival must come first and moreover that the two are separate entities. Rita warned 'we must be careful not to let the pandemic stop us progressing in gender or minority conversations' she felt it was all part of the same drive in 'helping our customers as well as employees and colleagues to balance in career and life'. Rita works tirelessly to raise awareness across the industry on this topic and invests time into the next generation through numerous mentoring programmes. Acknowledging that some businesses won't take this as an opportunity to 'reset their culture', she is vocal about how we can build better, more equitable, and productive environments during this time of change.

In Vanessa Vallely's closing statements, she spoke in depth about what a new normal workplace can look like, concluding that 'surely we don't shift back into this mad world of 8-6 and more and in the office everyday'. The presenteeism versus productivity debate is central to how businesses are looking to build their new normal following the pandemic, and in encouraging their workforce back to the office across the whole industry, we are seeing various 'hybrid' models being discussed as well as the extremes we previously spoke of at Goldman Sachs and their 95-hour work week. It will be interesting to see who takes advantage of this chance that we've been given to culture-create and which businesses decide to go back to what they know in expecting everyone in the office full-time with limited flexibility.

Just as COVID-19 has helped and hindered the mission in its own way, so has the UK Government's actions during the time of the pandemic. Having explained the gender pay gap statistics here in the UK, it couldn't be clearer how significant government support will be to affecting it. However, as previously stated gender pay gap reporting was abandoned during the pandemic undermining its importance and making it easier for firms to furlough working mothers, further infringing on their future career progression. All my work has been imploring businesses to take a stance on this in the absence of governmental support, even though it makes the mountain that much more a steeper climb. Without getting this right we are hindering our industry's ability to grow, and I fear walking into a future 'talent trap' where we won't be able to fullfill our goals without the 'women power' behind it. When discussing the maternity and paternity experience, many of my podcasts resulted in a call to action for the government. The government has a duty of care and duty to the economy to give workers better support during and after maternity and paternity leave, as well as better childcare support to encourage parents to return to work and be supported in doing so. As I write this, petitions are being signed to lobby the government on all these topics in hopes to drive enforceable change. Whilst we wait for this to take place many of the influencers across the industry continue to take action into their own hands. Joanne Dewar of Global Processing Systems, for example said, 'I have a responsibility to address the lack of diversity in its wider sense' and what she can affect was firstly by 'addressing the mechanisms in by which we recruit, performance assess, and promote'. Henna Ashraf, Head of Testing of Cashplus, a UK challenger bank, felt the same, 'I will continue supporting the aspiring generations because I wish there was someone to guide me in the early stages of my career'. Both women pointily reminding us of what we can all do to drive change. The change that is being driven is happening through individuals and now businesses. Imagine what we could do with governmental support too? This isn't to say the UK government are against helping businesses be more diverse and inclusive, they are simply not doing enough. There is for example, the 'Women in Finance Charter' which pledges a better gender balance across the industry. HM Treasury and signatory firms work together to ensure gender balance goals are set and worked towards and include promotional and pay on the senior executive team to be related to delivery on targets set. 330 businesses are signed up to this as of mid-2021 and they have all chosen to be part of it. The choice underlines that we need to drive this ourselves until the government truly step up.

Seema Khinda Johnson, Co-Founder of Nuggets, called for more too, 'I think the government should put their money where their mouth is and actually offer additional tax breaks to investors that back diverse teams and female founded businesses' arguing that this type of action would be a real driver for change. She like many others implore governmental support in making change happen through enforced policies. Seeing that without policy, people will continue to behave in the ways they always have done. They will pattern match and increase the divide between those that get funded and those they don't, essentially prolonging the problem.

Investors have a huge role to play too and have the ability to help or hinder the gender balance across FinTech and financial services. This gap simply can't be described as a gender imbalance but instead a gender precipice. The statistics as of mid-2021 have not shifted from the 2% we spoke of in previous chapters, however, some actions are being taken. Since more and more data is being produced providing evidence that female-led FinTechs produce higher revenues it's the investors that are making the connection between inclusion and success. Accelerator programmes are cropping up, as are female focused investing firms and venture partnerships to drive education and awareness across the investor community about how best to identify successful new ventures. Arshi Singh, the Head of Product at Comply Advantage, can see it happening, 'as far as the executive level goes, I think there is a push now from the investors'. She concluded that 'they want to see these boards comprising of more women, they want to see a certain percentage of the executive team consisting of more women' because they link that to better innovation, better profits, and overall success.

Roxane Sanguinetti is the head of fixed income and investor relations at GHCO, one of the fastest-growing liquidity providers specialising in exchange traded funds. The mission is to make financial markets transparent and accessible to all types of investors worldwide and as she says ETFs 'democratise access to investments for millions of people who don't have millions to invest'. Explaining that the likes of crowdfunding have opened opportunities for people who previously couldn't invest, Roxane works tirelessly to accelerate investment in businesses that don't fit the traditional male-led mould. She is certainly 'walking the talk' for improving the gender precipice in funding these female-led businesses by doing the investing herself. Roxane opened my eyes to how simple and accessible investing can be by sharing her own story of Angel Investing. She said, 'you can start with as little as a couple thousand pounds when you invest as part of a group'. She continued by saying, 'what's important is not the amount invested but the experience that you can bring to these start-ups. They may need expertise in your field from marketing to commercials or even access to your network'. One of her investments is an organisation called 50intech aiming for a 50% representation of women in Tech by 2050. She is yet another example of someone deciding to make the change themselves. Like my point on the government, we cannot keep waiting upon others to drive change, instead we must realise we all have our part to play and thanks to the democratisation of investing we all can.

In addition to this the Financial Times in early 2021 shared the brilliant news that goliath investment firm State Street would vote against directors of companies that fail to disclose their diversity figures of their board members. If the businesses that expect to be invested into don't have at least one 'minority' board member they would not receive investment. This will affect every single company in the FTSE 100 and many more too who rely on State Street as their 'top shareholder'. A bold move by an organisation big enough to demand huge amounts of change. Again, imagine if we saw more demands such as this? Change would happen far quicker than we have seen it, and everyone would have to 'walk the talk'. It is important to note we are seeing more of this type of action and in 2020 both Goldman Sachs and JP Morgan Chase launched initiatives to support female founders in their access to capital, support, and advisory services. Steps are being made and these bold moves need to be more commonplace to drive authentic change that will last.

Thinking about change that is sustainable, 'workplace authenticity' has become a huge theme within the industry as it has grown to the success it is today. This concept certainly has the potential to help us all affect the gender imbalance and wider diversity imbalance we face. We have witnessed a rise in people focus, people autonomy, diversity of thought, and empowerment which all paves the way for a more productive, successful, and inclusive workplace. Online forums and social reviews have made previous bad behaviour less possible as companies and managers can't act in ways they used to. As we all recognise the sheer potential of the FinTech space, so do leaders understand that they will need to just identify people who can do the job regardless of gender or any other diversity for that matter. Expanding the talent pool will have to be about enticing new and different people to our space and doing it in a way where we are appealing to them. As Lindsey Jayne, the VP of Product for Yoco, said quite rightly, 'there's plenty of abundance if you know how to create it' and furthermore attract it.

This has allowed for a rise in awareness from business leaders that if they don't tackle this authentically their business will suffer. Suresh Vaghjiani, Chief Executive Officer of Clowd 9, spoke about how to be a real success and to attract people for the long term, businesses 'need to go beyond what you can do for marketing'. He raised the hugely important issue that when 'logos have turned to the rainbow clouds or you're posting a quote on Black Lives Matter', it must be genuine and have policies and procedures that truly back this or clients and customers will eventually see through this. Claire Norman is the Head of Financial Crime at Jaja Finance, a FinTech on a mission to redefine and simplify the credit card experience. She also felt strongly about the issue of authenticity citing that 'lots of companies advertise that they are diverse and inclusive, then you turn up and it's not the case and it was a tick box exercise'. She is a massive believer in company values being central to policy and that senior leadership and C suite staff have a duty to be true to those values through their culture. She summarised, 'people are wising up and want to see evidence' of accepting cultures that allow people to thrive and they aren't joining firms who can't give proof at the rate they used to.

The good news is that, according to Sangeetha Narasimham of Mambu, 'people are willing to change'. She gave me lots of confidence as she recounted seeing people responding well to the change needed in their own behaviour to make this industry better. Talking specifically about how people had started to seek out feedback and to reframe their own methods of hiring, promotions and people focused decision-making to be more equitable for all. Couple this sentiment with what Mary Agbesanwa of PWC highlighted, again I feel excited about the potential for huge steps forward. Mary said, 'more young people than ever are passionate about FinTech and understanding financial services' and that potential 'talent is evenly distributed, but opportunities are not'. With this growth in company action and the need for authentically inclusive environments, 'evenly distributed' opportunities are becoming more and more commonplace. Our mission is to make it more so than ever before.

Every point I have raised has the potential to help or hinder the drive towards authentic workplace inclusion of which the gender balance is a part of. I always remind myself of Henna Ashraf's words when I think of the sheer magnitude of the mission we are on, when she so poignantly said within her career and facing the challenges she faced as a woman in technology 'I could be pitiful or powerful and I chose powerful'. My closing statements will reflect Henna, whose words inspire me every day.

11

Be Powerful

In all these pages my mission has been to take you on an inclusion journey to open your eyes to the real challenges we face when trying to tackle the gender imbalance in the FinTech and wider workplace. I felt that showing you how passionate I am about the wonderful industry I work in and its potential for such an abundance of change really puts us in the greatest position to become trailblazers in the drive for gender equality in the workplace. For this to happen I wanted to honestly highlight the barriers we need to break before change can happen. I did this through talking about 'the system' we currently work within and then 'the foundations' I believe we need to reset. I showed how the good steps we have made, have sadly failed to reach a 'tipping point' and more importantly how they could if we all contribute to that change. Not only have I showcased the actions needed but also what we must demand from the higher bodies to allow for the results we desire. Intrinsically we know that this industry can drive more profits and in turn a wider economy, if run to its true potential and when authentic inclusion is realised, we can begin tapping at that door. As Laura Rofe of PPRO put it, investors, leaders, and C suite executives cannot turn a blind eye to the fact that 'powerful women lead to powerful returns'. I believe we must open our eyes to connecting inclusion to the future success of our businesses as a first step to ensure change happens.

All the lessons, the learns, and the direction have come from the amazing individuals I feel privileged to have been able to interview across my podcast series and I cannot wait for the many more I will speak to across this industry

© The Author(s), under exclusive license to Springer Nature
Switzerland AG 2022
N. Edwards-Dashti, *FinTech Women Walk the Talk*,
https://doi.org/10.1007/978-3-030-90574-3_11

as the movement intensifies. I am truly inspired by what I have learnt and incredibly optimistic about what we can do as an industry especially since witnessing the sheer volume and pace of change in early 2021. As Akita Somani of Elavon so rightly pointed out, 'often we have the right intent' but the industry doesn't know how to implement change. I felt compelled to give the blueprint to more than just our industry on what needs to be done to allow for a better workplace balance. I haven't only been driven by my own experience but more so of the visibility I have across this huge marketplace and the relationships I have cultivated that allow me to share the wise words of all the women and their allies that are constantly 'walking the talk' for change daily in their careers.

Similarly, to how the FinTech industry blossomed after the 2008 financial crisis, COVID-19 and its disruption to the business environment could help 'level the playing field' and offer a host of new opportunities for women entrepreneurs. I refuse to overlook the devastation COVID-19 has ensued on people worldwide and that drives me forward in ensuring that in our space in particular we do not disrespect the chance we have been given. With the new level of people awareness, the opportunity to build more inclusive environments is in our hands to utilise or squander. Lax Naryan of Toronto Dominion Securities once said, 'we were in a phase where we were diversity blind, and it wasn't discussed and now we are in a very diversity brave environment where everyone is talking about it, everyone is aware of it and we are doing things about it'. These actions we are now taking are the responsibilities of us all and I have wanted to showcase in these pages how everyone has their part to play. This sentiment was driven by the conversation I had with Sara Green Brodersen, multiple business Founder. She had said, 'It's not a problem we can solve by one actor doing one thing. it has to be a holistic approach' and everyone needs to be included from investors, to managers, to executives, and peers. Everyone has the potential to be an ally, and everyone should choose to be an ally, since addressing the gender imbalance in the workplace will make us all more successful in the long run.

Thea Fisher felt that as an industry there is a huge opportunity in the fact that 'FinTech is a nascent sector so there's not necessarily a background that's perfect for it'. Acknowledging that both finance and technology are traditionally very non-diverse sectors she did feel that this cycle could be broken by new ways of thinking and FinTech's ability to challenge the status quo. Also, we cannot overlook the rise of diversity of thought and what that has encouraged in business leaders in their pursuit to build better products for an ever-evolving marketplace of consumer. Leda Gyliptis of 10x Banking proclaimed, 'I need people who will ask questions I don't expect' and the more she gets the better she knows her business and its products will be. Another angle on this same point came from Georgia Stewart the Chief Executive Officer of Tumelo who said, 'FinTech is not an industry where you need to hire someone from finance. It's an industry where you need people who can think differently, disrupt the system, care about the end customer, and have strong values around progress'. Georgia's business Tumelo has revolutionised investment and pension platforms by transforming ESG into positive retention, acquisition, and brand opportunities and her business has grown through hiring people in line with her statement.

We need to see more C-level executives 'walking the talk' to allow for more successes here. Serena Koivurinta of Caplin reminds us that she came from 'a business and marketing background and people from these backgrounds have huge potential within our space and shouldn't be neglected'. In the early parts of this book, I highlighted many examples like these to outline the importance of us building the industry with people potential from all sorts of backgrounds and not waiting for the STEM applicants to come through. Parallel to this we looked at how we can all get involved in 'next generation inspiration' to change societal perceptions so we can attract more people to STEM. As Monika Gupta of Decimal Factor said, 'talent has no gender, race or age' and we can build incredible teams if we only allow ourselves to see this point through acknowledging the change needed in ourselves.

Claire Norman of Jaja Finance was clear in her closing statement, 'we need huge changes in society otherwise women will always be overlooked and underestimated' and there is a lot we can all do to put pressure on investors to see the 'powerful returns', on the government through lobbying for better childcare provisions and through how we educate and nurture the next generation. Sophie Guibard of OpenPayd was speaking to me about her journey into motherhood and having a career when she said, 'you don't have to be a Wonder Woman, it takes some concessions and a strong supporting network made up of family, made of carers and a very strong partner - I don't want to look like the woman that does everything because I have a lot of people supporting me and without it I wouldn't be able to do it'. We all need to feel more supported and within a society of better balance to allow for the true potential of success and its returns to take place. Evgenia Loginova of Radar Payments spoke of the importance of addressing the next generation issue however long term this may be saying, 'It is upon us to ensure that we educate and encourage women very early on to include math and science into their career options. The next wave of technology is all about a digital life with AI around data, sharing and consent'. She is an avid believer in STEM and what modern-day technologists actually require and that being 'skill sets and a leadership style that heavily leans towards ethics, collaboration and transparency, which tend to fit very well with female talent'. We must insist on driving this forward alongside all the other work to allow for an influx of technologists into the industry for years to come. This is not a task for other people to take a lead on and the work needed here is for everyone to work with schools, universities, their families, and friends to dispel the tradition gendered perspectives around the STEM.

The Henna Ashraf motto of "choose powerful" rings true when Julie Ashmore of Rapid Cash shared a wonderful story about her daughter at nine years of age. She had once said to her daughter, "don't let anyone tell you can't do something because you are a girl," and in response her daughter questioned, "what do you mean mum?" Julie went on to explain how vividly she remembered that moment saying, "that resonated with me, and I suddenly thought we have a whole generation growing up and no matter what shape, size, religion or background they come from they have the opportunity and that's what I'd like the future to be." The next generation are demanding more, expecting more, and in their perceptions of what is fair in the world will allow for the change some of us are paving to solidify.

I have wanted to share what I have seen across the two decades I have worked in this industry and what I know works within businesses to make them stronger. Similarly, I wanted to be honest about the female experience in the workplace as I believe, when we acknowledge the truth only then can we move forward and break down the barriers. Everyone needs to take part and be powerful in driving the mission to balance gender in our workplaces.

To truly 'choose powerful' I think of the joy of Monica Millares when she proclaimed, 'If only one person speaks up, we only have the value of one person' and 'I add my value because I am different!' We all have a responsibility to bring our differences to this movement and drive change. This is a call to action to those who don't see the gender imbalance as their fight as I believe we must all ignite the real ally within us and act upon it.

This industry is about change and if we 'choose to be powerful' we can make the changes needed for a better and more inclusive and therefore successful workplace. Even looking back to the challenges, I openly shared for the female experience I am incredibly driven to attract more women to this space because I know we are closing in on the tipping point where we can invest in people, build their careers, and teach them things to allow for real empowerment to take place.

The women of FinTech and their allies within the pages of this book have done nothing but inspire me, support me, teach me, and help me grow confidence to tackle this mission. I am so excited to share their lessons as I know many people will want to join this wonderful industry having now seen how many powerful, creative, innovative women are within it already. The bigger picture is for how as an industry we can show the entire world what we are capable of and how parity has the potential of being achieved. There is still much work to be done and I cannot disregard the wider perception problem we all face in the societal barriers regarding women's capabilities, women in leadership, working mothers, and gendered stereotypes. This is where FinTech has a huge potential in breaking down these barriers and debunking these age-old myths that propagate the gendered struggle for parity.

I know that the FinTech career journey is an exciting one that is open to all, with missions, values, and purpose that will engage people, inspire people, and help people become the best they can be. I have no doubt that together we will take all the themes I have covered well past the tipping point and drive a movement if only we choose to.

By picking up this book I know 'papering over the cracks' will be reduced. I have wanted to inspire everyone to be a part of the movement of change and this book should have provided you your very own blueprint. I believe focusing on fundamental foundation change will start to happen if the genuine desire is there to give your team or business its best chance to succeed. We will see this in the implementation of action from allies to bias champions, to committees, to adequate demographic measurement, promotional criteria, to continued education, and its follow-up as we know these actions pave the way for success. Even more so if they are built on the foundations of psychological safety, parental policies, mechanisms to address the overlooked, gender pay gap erasure, and the all-important management backing in policy to enable procedure and its daily implementation. With just some of these highlights in place we will see the results we desire.

I don't deny the challenge, but I'm excited by the possibility of many more of us 'walking the talk'. I leave you with Irene Perdomo, Managing Director of Gresham Investment Management, a multimillion pound investment firm, whose journey was such a weaving path of challenge that I named her podcast 'the against all odds' episode. Her voice is in my mind when I continue to drive this movement. When I see a challenge, I am reminded of her when she said, 'I'm too stubborn to listen to rejection, they tell me no and I say let's go for it!'

It's time we all go for it together and 'walk the talk'.

Index